S0-BOF-934

Behold the Christ:
Getting *to Know the Heart and Mind of Jesus Christ from Psalm 119*

by Richard L. Routh

Behold the Christ:
Getting *to Know the Heart and Mind of Jesus Christ from Psalm 119*

by Richard L. Routh

Copyright © 2018 by Richard L. Routh, All Rights Reserved, 2nd edition.

*Scripture quotations taken from the **HOLY BIBLE, NEW INTERNATIONAL VERSION**. Copyright © 1973, 1978, 1984 by International Bible Society. Used by permission of Zondervan Publishing House.*

Note: When quoting the NIV text, the Hebrew Tetragrammaton, transliterated into English as YHWH, has been used instead of the words "O LORD" and "LORD." When the NIV scholars came across the Hebrew Tetragrammaton in the original Hebrew text, they translated it "O LORD" or "LORD" as is the common and accepted practice in modern English translations. However, because this Psalm is considered a prayer of Jesus being prayed to His Father (YHWH), and since LORD is often used throughout the NIV to refer to any member of the God-head (Father, Son, Holy Spirit, or all three at one time), in order to help reduce ambiguity, this book has reinserted the original Hebrew in its transliterated form: YHWH. This only increases the accuracy of the English verses because YHWH is the transliterated word the Psalmist used.

Author's convention: The author holds the Scriptures in very high regard, acknowledging it to be the spoken word of God. In recognition of this, he has chosen to capitalize the following words in the "Meditations and commentary" portions of this book: Command(s), Law(s), Precept(s), Statutes, Testimonies, Decrees, Judgments, and Ordinances, when they are referring to the written word of God as contained in the Scriptures. (The exception to this convention is that the word "word" is not capitalized, even when it is referring to the Scriptures, because the capital form, the "Word" of God, refers to Christ—a name used to refer to Him in the Gospel of John and other places in the Scriptures.) No particular meaning should be attached to this convention other than it is the author's preference as a sign of high regard.

Dedication: For Edie, Daniel, Amber, Anne, Evan, Thomas Stephen, Heather, David, Gracely, Grace and ?, my God-Son Samuel Wood and his friend Jenny, and all of my grandchildren. I wrote this book mostly for you, but I don't mind if everyone else reads it, also.

Acknowledgement and special thanks go to Dr. Steven D. Caldwell for his patient mentoring over the past several years and for directing me to many of the key thematic Scriptural cross references that appear throughout the commentary in this book.

Table of Contents

Behold the Christ   Copyright © 2018, Richard L. Routh, All rights reserved.   6

Chapter One: Introduction

Expect to be greatly surprised, delighted, and renewed by what you learn about Jesus as you prayerfully meditate on what you discover here the verses of Psalm 119.

I am old, so I've been around a long time. I've been ardently seeking and following the Lord for the past four and half decades. For many of those years I made it a daily habit in the mornings to rise early and pray through a psalm. I would start with Psalm 1, and about 150 days later, finally get to Psalm 150, and then I would start all over again. Since I usually prayed one line of a psalm at a time, followed by a discussion with God about what it meant and what it meant to me and what He wanted me to see there, it was not unusual that it might take me an hour or more to pray through a psalm. When I would get to Psalm 119, I would wince and usually hurry through it because it was so long, and frankly, (although I would not want to say this out loud so anyone could hear me) boring.

If I am speaking frankly and honestly, there was another bothering reason I tended to shy away from Psalm 119. I am a huge advocate of the doctrines of Grace. My favorite book in the Bible was Galatians. My most valued book outside the Bible is *Martin Luther's Commentary on Galatians* (just right ahead of J.I. Packer's book, *Knowing God*). Some verses that give me great comfort are passages such as Hebrews 8:13, "By calling this covenant 'new,' he has made the first one obsolete; and what is obsolete and aging will soon disappear" and Colossians 2:14, "having cancelled the written code, with its regulations, that was against us and that stood opposed to us; he took it away, nailing it to the cross." And then there were the places where Paul made it clear that the Law of Moses kills us (like Second Corinthians 3:6). So, why would I want to spend much time focusing on Psalm 119 which is a very long section of the Old Testament that I assumed talked exclusively about the benefits of the Law/Commands/Precepts/Statutes of the Old Covenant (as given by Moses)? Why would I want to look intently into something that was obsolete and killed me? I didn't. (Although I did not really know what to do with that nagging statement of Jesus in Matthew 5:18-19, where He says, "I tell you the truth, until heaven and earth disappear, not the smallest letter, not the least stroke of a pen, will by any means disappear from the Law until everything is accomplished. Anyone who breaks one of the least of these commandments and teaches others to do the same will be called least in the kingdom of heaven, but whoever practices and teaches these commands will be called great in the kingdom of heaven." I had various theologically sound ways of explaining away this statement, or at least diminishing the obvious emphatic value Jesus placed on it, but it was still a nagging passage.)

And then a few years back, I was fervently praying to Jesus asking Him if He would reveal to me what His daily prayer life was like. I had learned that if you really want to know someone, study His prayer life when no one is listening. At least I knew that was the way it worked for me, and I had heard others say pretty much the same thing. So, the reason I was requesting this was to get to know Him better. (I was seeking to follow the "advice" in John 17:3.) I knew from New Testament passages that Jesus often would go to a secluded spot early in the morning and pray. So, my request was, "Lord, would you tell me what you prayed about during those times?"

The Holy Spirit clearly impressed me to delve deeper into Psalm 119 and I would find the answer to my question there. I have spent just about every day for the past few years prayerfully pondering Psalm 119 with Christ, and asking Him a lot of questions about why He prayed each verse, one octet per day. Psalm 119 has 22 octets, so it would usually take me a little less than a month to get all the way through Psalm 119 like this, and then I would start it all over again. I estimate I have prayed all the way through Psalm 119 this way about 40 times. Each time, the Holy Spirit revealed new and deeper insights into the person of Jesus Christ and the person of YHWH. It never got old. Eventually, I had learned so much about Jesus from this exercise, that I felt compelled to share some of those insights with others. Hence, this book.

Why You Might Want to Read this Book

Many books allow the reader to read the first chapter, or sometimes the last chapter, to get most of the main points written about in the book. This book is not like that.

Nowhere in this book is there a summary of the main points of Psalm 119. The very nature of Psalm 119 does not allow for the constructing of such a list that would not be grossly misunderstood.

So, the reader may ask, why should I read this book? What is the value in this book to me?

Here are some of the at least 176 very good reasons to read this book:

- You will get to **personally know Jesus Christ and His Father** probably **much** better than you did before you read this book.

- If you went back in time 2,000 years to the dusty roads of Galilee and Judea, and had an opportunity to walk beside Jesus, and ask Him any of these questions, what would His answers be?
    - "Lord, what are you thinking about right now?" (Hint: The answer is ALWAYS the same.)
    - "Lord, what is it in life that you are most passionate about?"
    - "Lord, is it a difficult burden to keep all the Laws of God without ever messing up?"
    - "Lord, do you get your understanding, insight, and wisdom the same way I do?"
    - "Lord, have you ever performed a miracle to reduce the pain and discomfort you felt in the midst of any trial you faced?" (In other words, "Have You ever used Your God-powers to make Your life easier? Or were you actually hurt in all the same ways I am hurt in my life?")
    - "Lord, how do you emotionally process excruciating pain and disappointment in your life?"
    - "Lord, what do you feel when others try to trick you into doing wrong things?"
    - "Lord, exactly **how** is it that by You obeying all the Laws of God and then dying for my sin, does that accomplish my righteousness? I mean, I know it does, but I don't understand HOW it works. Can you explain that to me?"

o "Lord, what do you think about the idea of trying to get smarter and smarter by using computers to analyze lots and lots of data? I mean, it seems like it should work, but often those who base big decisions on that approach seem to make some of the most colossal mistakes. Why is that? Am I missing something here?"

o "Lord, you say that eternal life is experientially knowing the Father and You. So, I definitely want to do that. Please tell me, how do I **best** get to really know You better?"

You might guess at the answer to the above questions based on your understanding of other passages in Scripture, but a careful study of Psalm 119 unequivocally reveals the answers to all the above questions, as well as at least 100 more.

Additionally: If you struggle, as many do, with how to balance God's Grace and God's Law, then you need to read this book. After you have digested the insights Jesus gives us in Psalm 119, you will not struggle with that question again. You will clearly see how they fit together without contradicting each other. You will clearly see how each works to strengthen and exalt the other, as opposed to a common notion that they are in some sort of tension with each other.

Challenge to Reader

Based on what I learned as I studied this psalm, I can now see a strong, compelling case based on many evidences contained in the Psalm 119, that this was indeed the daily prayer of Christ. In Chapter Three of this book, and scattered throughout the commentary in this book, are highlighted many evidences to support this conclusion. The reader does not have to take my word for this, but look at the evidence and let the Lord convict you of this.

How to Make Best Use of this Book: So, are you willing to spend 10 minutes per day getting to know Jesus Christ and His Father better? After reading the first three chapters, I challenge you to go through this book, as part of your daily devotional, one verse at a time. I recommend you follow this pattern:

1. Read a verse in both the NIV and the Hebrew Literal and try to identify any differences that might be there.
2. Say to Jesus, "Lord, why did you pray this verse:" then recite the verse back to Jesus and wait for Him to guide your thoughts in answer to your question.
3. Then after spending a minute or two listening for the Holy Spirit to answer your question, read the "Meditations and commentary" section associated with that verse.
4. Beginning at verse 57, you will also be asked a question (or two) at the end of each commentary. Take a minute to write out your answer to that question in the space provided.
5. Some people progress at the rate of only one verse per day. Which is fine. Some people try to do four verses per day. Some people try to do eight verses per day if time allows.

You probably don't want to attempt more than 8 verses (an octet) in a single devotional time.

If you accept this challenge, and see it all the way to the end, I assure you that you will be glad you did! Thank you for taking this challenge!

Behold the Christ   Copyright © 2018, Richard L. Routh, All rights reserved.   10

Chapter Two: Part of the Mission of the Christ

In Genesis chapters one and two, we see **God providing** a world that was **"very good"** for people to enjoy and rule over. The emphasis in these two chapters is that "God provides good through His spoken word." The good world God provided was characterized by glorious beauty, no death or disease, no sorrow, everything working in harmony, and people walking in close fellowship with God.

In Genesis 3:1-7, Satan brings a counter proposition to our first parents. He proposes that people, not God, should be the ones to decide what is good and what is not. When Adam and Eve chose to accept this proposition, the world fell—which is to say, the trajectory of history took a sharp left turn and left the path of light and life that God had originally intended for it through His decrees and provision. Death entered the world because of their decision (Romans 5:12). Sorrow, disease, and dissention now became the norm and the close fellowship with God was rejected and set aside.

Jesus Christ came to redeem and restore this fallen world and its sinful people. To do so, one of the things He needed to do was to start back where the thread of history was broken. As the second Adam, He had to reverse the decision made by Adam and demonstrate the reasonableness and desirability of the plan originally intended by God, namely that God would be the one to decide what is good and what is not, and to reestablish that **through God's decrees of what is good, and what is not, God would be the one to provide goodness to people**. Therefore, a big part of the redemption of people and their fallen world was to demonstrate the viability of a life lived according to God's Plan A—which was a repudiation of Satan's Plan B.

This prayer of Christ in Psalm 119 chronicles the struggles Jesus Christ had with people committed to Plan B, while He was living a life according to Plan A. As we read Psalm 119, we see Christ frequently crying out against the beliefs and practices of people who are committed to deciding for themselves how they should live their lives, especially when those beliefs and practices conflict with His commitment to live His life completely dependent on, and in accordance with, the provisions of YHWH as declared in the Decrees of YHWH (as they appear in the written Scriptures).

This conflict between lives lived as people see best (ALL the people among whom Jesus lived) versus a life lived exclusively according to the Laws of YHWH was an epic struggle of enormous proportion and eternal consequence. Jesus' life was the **quintessential threat** to the proposition that one could decide for himself or herself what was best, and it was perceived as such, especially by the powerbrokers of the time.

Brief Summary of Satan's proposition to Eve

1. Satan said to Eve, "You will not die." The implication of this statement was that the physical part of her existence was more important (valid) than the spiritual part of her existence. By rejecting God's authority in favor of her own, she was rejecting the source of her spiritual life, and therefore, she was committing spiritual suicide.

2. Satan said to Eve, "Your eyes will be opened." The implication of this statement was that: What **YOU** see is what counts. What **YOU** perceive to be true is more valid than what you might think God has said is true. Therefore, you should become reliant on what you observe (in the physical world) and what you can infer from those observations.

3. Satan said to Eve, "You will be like God, knowing good and evil." The implication of this statement: It is not good for God to be in the place to dictate to you what is good and what is not. Instead of being dependent on God for all your perceptions and judgments, you will be better off if you are the one to be able to judge for yourself what is important and what is not. It will be better for you if you are the one to decide what is good (fair) and what is evil (not fair). Don't you want to have the right to decide what is fair? Do you really want someone else, God in this case, to be able to dictate to you what it fair? Doesn't your opinion count? Yes, you are important enough for your opinion to count. Assert your independence! Show them that you count for something and that you are important!

The Activities of Psalm 119

The temptation of Christ in the wilderness as recorded in Matthew 4:1-4 is a reassertion of Satan's original proposition to Eve. If Satan could get Jesus to rely on Himself instead of on the provisions of YHWH as revealed in His word (which is a picture of YHWH's very person), then all would be lost for us. If Satan could have gotten Jesus to use His own divine powers to satisfy his legitimate and extreme hunger needs, then the proposition that Satan made to Eve would have still stood, and God's "proposition" to provide all our needs from His gracious generosity through His word would have continued to be repudiated. Jesus was the second/last Adam. And as such, Jesus, by choosing NOT to use His own divine powers to alleviate His suffering and satisfy His need ("Man shall not live by bread alone, but by every word that proceeds from the mouth of God"), was effectively repudiating Satan's proposition—and we are to take note of that!

This, then, is part of the motivation and mission of the incarnate Christ—to repudiate the proposition of Satan, namely: that we should be the ones to decide when and how to cause "good" to happen. Jesus was here, at least in part, to demonstrate that it is a reasonable, even preferred, path through life to rely exclusively on the provisions of YHWH as revealed to us through His word. Chronicling and demonstrating what that looks like is what Psalm 119 is all about.

*To read more about the author's thoughts on Satan's proposition to abandon God's law and its implications, and Jesus' rebuttal to this proposition and the reestablishment of God's original proposition, see the Appendix A: "Musings of the Author on The Mission of the Christ."

Chapter Three: The Purpose, Structure and Flow of Psalm 119

Some Psalms are Messianic

The psalms were written about 1000 years before the birth of Christ. Some psalms are clearly and widely accepted as being "messianic" psalms. This means they are either prophetic of some aspect of the life of the incarnate Christ, or they are (will be) the actual words that will be spoken by Christ.

An example (there are many) of where a psalm is prophetic of something about the life of Christ is, "YHWH has sworn and will not change his mind: 'You are a priest forever, in the order of Melchizedek'" (Psalm 110:4), which is confirmed as being fulfilled by Christ in Hebrews 5:6, "And he says in another place, 'You are a priest forever, in the order of Melchizedek,'" and in Hebrews 6:20: "where our forerunner, Jesus, has entered on our behalf. He has become a high priest forever, in the order of Melchizedek."

An example (there are many) of where a psalm records the actual words that will be spoken by Christ is in Psalm 22, "My God, my God, why have you forsaken me?" These same words were spoken by Jesus on the cross at His death as recorded in Matthew 27:46. In case one is tempted to think these words in Psalm 22 are being taken out of context, a thorough reading of the rest of Psalm 22 establishes this context by painting a vivid picture of several aspects of the crucifixion of Jesus Christ (which also makes this a messianic psalm).

It is commonly accepted that some psalms are messianic and contain the actual words of Christ, even though those words will not be spoken by Christ for another 1000 years after the writing of the psalm. The question here is, "Is Psalm 119 one of these messianic psalms?"

Psalm 119 was the daily prayer of Jesus Christ

The authorship of this psalm is unknown, except that we believe it to be the words of the Holy Spirit (the Spirit of Christ), as are all the psalms and all of Scripture. So why do we say that Psalm 119 is the prayer of Christ? There are several reasons. Some of the things claimed by the Psalmist could only be claimed by Christ. Some of the roles and responsibilities claimed by the Psalmist could only be shouldered by Christ. Many of the commitments expressed by the Psalmist could only be fulfilled by Christ. If you are skeptical about this assertion, then please keep an open mind about the possibility and by the end of this book, I suspect you will be solidly convinced that not only is this indeed a prayer of Christ, but it could not be the prayer of anyone else.

The argument for this being the continual *daily* prayer of Christ is made in the commentary following verses 148 and 164.

Claims that Only Christ Could Make

There are many claims made throughout Psalm 119 that could only be made by Jesus Christ. Anyone else attempting to make these claims, especially in the face of the Thrice Holy Lord God Almighty who sees all things, would at best be delusional and completely self-deceived. For example, the Psalmist makes the following claims; claims that cannot be true of us if we are to be qualified to seek salvation through the blood of Christ, and claims that MUST be true of the One who's blood provides that salvation:

- "Though the arrogant have smeared me with lies, **I keep your precepts with all my heart**." (v. 69)
- "The arrogant mock me without restraint, but **I do not turn from your law**." (v. 51)
- "My soul is consumed with longing for your laws **at all times**." (v. 20)
- "**I hold fast to your statutes**, O Lord ; do not let me be put to shame." (v. 31)

There are many other such examples throughout Psalm 119. These are just four of them. In fact, there are so many such claims made throughout this psalm (and the claims often appear as the basis for which the help of YHWH is being claimed) that one must conclude the psalmist was either hopelessly delusional and arrogant, or the Psalmist must be Christ.

Commitments that Only Christ Could Fulfill and Responsibilities that Only Christ Could Shoulder

Some of the commitments made by the Psalmist in this psalm are extraordinary. They are promises the Psalmist makes to YHWH, and these promises are often made as the foundation upon which the blessings and deliverance that will come from YHWH are to be predicated. As such, the Psalmist is laying out the basis for the justification of the Church which is to be secured by His obedience. Christ's commitments are as follows:

- "You are my portion, O Lord ; I have promised to obey your words." (v. 57)
- "I have taken an oath and confirmed it, that I will follow your righteous laws." (v. 106)
- "Give me understanding, and I will keep your law and obey it with all my heart." (v. 34)
- "I will never forget your precepts, For by them you have preserved [revived] my life." (v. 93)
- ""I will always obey your law, for ever and ever." (v. 44)
- "I will speak of your statutes before kings and I will not be put to shame." (v. 46)
- The entire Mem octet (vv. 97-104)

The Structure and Flow of Psalm 119

Psalm 119 is the longest chapter in the Bible. It is a prayer to YHWH—all 176 verses. It is organized into 22 different 8-verse groupings. Each of these 8-verse groupings is commonly referred to as an "octet."

Furthermore, this Psalm is an acrostic in the original Hebrew language. Specifically, the first octet is called the Aleph octet, because the first word of each of the eight verses in this octet begins with the letter Aleph (in the Hebrew). Aleph is also the first letter of the Hebrew alphabet. It is also the Hebrew symbol for the number one.

The second octet is called the Beth octet, because the first word of each of the eight verses in this octet begins with the letter Beth. And, yes, you guessed it, Beth is the second letter of the Hebrew alphabet. Beth is also the Hebrew symbol for the number two.

In the third octet, all the first words of each of the eight verses begin with Gimel, the third letter of the alphabet, and also the Hebrew symbol for the number 3. And so forth, all the way to last letter Taw, the 22nd letter of the 22-letter Hebrew alphabet. 22 octets makes for 176 verses.

The nature of an acrostic, by its very structure, tends to focus attention on the acrostic words. So the Hebrew student who was memorizing this Psalm, would tend to remember each verse based on the first word of each verse. Therefore, the first word of each verse would be of primary focus, or at least have extra emphasis for that verse. To help the reader be able to follow this emphasis, the Hebrew literal is provided along with each verse in the NIV. Hebrew grammar allows for the compounding and enhanced conjugation of words more so than English typically does. The result is that often one of these verses consists of only five or six Hebrew words, whereas its English translation may contain twice that many words, or more. In this book, each Hebrew word is underlined with a single underline. For example, the second verse in the English NIV is, "Blessed are they who keep his statutes and seek him with all their heart." This verse contains 14 English words. The Hebrew for this verse contains only six words. The first word in the Hebrew is " 'asre" which is translated into the English in the NIV as "Blessed are" and the second Hebrew word for this verse is "nosere" which is translated into the English in the NIV as "they who keep," and so forth. The Hebrew literal, as printed in this book, shows the Hebrew word boundaries by the use of the underline. So, all three words "they who keep" are underlined with a single underline showing that they are all one word in the Hebrew.

Another structural characteristic is that each octet has its own theme. Some themes are quickly obvious. For example, most readers will notice that the Kaph octet is all about dealing with excruciating pain and suffering. Other octets have a more subtle theme that takes a good bit of study and cross referencing between verses to spot the theme of that octet. Understanding the theme of an octet helps to establish the context for better ferreting out the role each verse plays in establishing that theme and in providing a richer perspective on that theme.

In addition to each octet having its own theme, these themes, when they are connected in sequence, form a trajectory that tells the story of a relationship between a man and God. To see this story become the context for the relationship between the incarnate Christ and His Father is where there is enormous value in studying this psalm.

In the context of that trajectory, this psalm is a passionate prayer filled with crying out in pain, crying out in celebratory praise, petition, resolution, and the entire spectrum of human emotion. To see how Jesus Christ lived His life through these passions is the primary purpose of this book.

א Aleph (1) – Theme: The importance of having the right desire

1. "Blessed are they whose ways are blameless,
   who walk according to the law of the YHWH." (NIV)

   Hebrew Literal: "<u>The blessed [are]</u>   <u>blameless</u>   <u>in their ways</u>
                    <u>Who walk</u>   <u>in the law</u>   <u>of YHWH</u>."

   Meditations and commentary:

   - These first two octets (vv. 1-16) comprise a sort of introduction where Jesus states His intent and proclaims the main themes of what and how He will run this race of His incarnation. In these two octets He is proclaiming the ways and means whereby He will accomplish His mission, which is in part, demonstrating the reasonableness of God's proposition that He should be the One who declares what is good (in contrast to Satan's proposition to Adam and Eve in Genesis 3:1-7).

   - Jesus, in this His prayer to His Father, YHWH, is extolling blamelessness. He says it comes (to Him) through walking according to the word/Law of YHWH, but a lot of things come from walking according to the word of YHWH. That is, a lot of character claims can be made of anyone (although there has only ever been Jesus Christ) who consistently (without fail) walk according to the Law of YHWH. So, what does it mean to be blameless and why start this monumental psalm, this longest prayer in Scripture,--why start it off by focusing on blamelessness? Why such a big deal about being blameless?

     I do not think Jesus, at least as an adult, ever lost a continual conscious awareness that the reason for His incarnation was to be the pure unblemished Lamb of God who would be the propitiatory sacrifice for our sin so that we, the Church His bride, would be redeemed (John 12:27).

     For Jesus, achieving and maintaining blamelessness was missional. And in this verse, He proclaims the truth that being blameless is predicated on walking according to the Law of YHWH. He is saying (among other things) in this first verse, "Father (YHWH), in order for me to accomplish my mission, the mission for which You sent me, then I must remain blameless, which means I must continually walk in accordance with Your Law (as it was spoken by You in the Scriptures)."

     In other words, Jesus is recognizing, proclaiming, and as we shall see more about this later in this psalm, pleading with His Father for His help in ensuring Jesus is successful in His incarnate mission by constantly walking in accordance with the Law of YHWH. This is the theme of this entire psalm and Jesus begins by proclaiming it in this first verse.

2. "Blessed are they who keep his statutes
   and seek him with all their heart." (NIV)

   Hebrew Literal: "Blessed [are]   they who keep   His testimonies
                   [who] with all   their heart   seek him."

   Meditations and commentary:

   • Here Jesus continues to elaborate on the theme He began in v. 1. It was not enough to be "obedient" to the Law of YHWH by ensuring that His actions conform with the Laws of YHWH (as given in the Scriptures), but it was necessary that He seek the face of YHWH with all His heart. Jesus is recognizing here in v. 2 that walking in the Law of YHWH (v. 1), keeping the testimonies of YHWH (v. 2), are predicated on seeking YHWH with all His heart. It was not just a behavior thing, it was crucially a heart thing.

   • These first few verses of Psalm 119 are introducing themes that will be unpacked as this prayer unfolds throughout the rest of this psalm.

3. "They do nothing wrong;
   they walk in his ways." (NIV)

   Hebrew Literal: "They also   not   do do   iniquity
                   in his ways   they walk."

   Meditations and commentary:

   • What is iniquity? (See the Hebrew Literal for this verse.) Its original meaning comes from the idea of inequality. An action/behavior is iniquitous when it stems from an errant understanding of what is right or just or fair in God's sight. In other words, it is an unbalanced view, a twisting, a perversion of what should be good.

When we think about iniquity, we think about the ugly and unspeakable behaviors from the seamy and disturbing side of life. Iniquity is sordid and degrading to those who do it and to those who view it.

When we accept Satan's proposition to determine what is good (see Genesis 3:1-7), when we reject God's declaration of what good looks like in favor of figuring it out for ourselves, then iniquity is the inevitable, inescapable result.

Therefore, the proactive inoculation against iniquity, as well as its antidote and remedy once infected, is to reject Satan's proposition that we can figure this out on our own, and instead, wholeheartedly and enthusiastically embrace the accurate understandings of what good looks like as they are laid out for us by God in His Testimonies and His Law (as He has done in the Scriptures).

As we shall see in greater detail later in this psalm, Jesus was deeply grieved and oppressed by the iniquity that pervaded the lives of those around Him. And for Jesus, the Testimonies of YHWH as contained in the Scriptures were a source of light in this darkness; they were a source of solid hope in this environment of despair; they were a source of comfort and celebration in the face of great perversion and pain.

As Jesus prays these words in v. 3 to His Father (YHWH), He is finding solace, hope, strength and light for His soul in the fact that iniquity is avoided when one walks in the ways of YHWH.

4. "You have laid down precepts
   that are to be fully obeyed." (NIV)

   Hebrew Literal: "You   have ordained   your precepts
                        to be kept   diligently."

Meditations and commentary:

- In this verse Jesus is declaring that the Precepts of YHWH are to be kept diligently. YHWH has ordained that they are to be kept with complete consistency—that is to say, YHWH's Precepts are to be kept without ever slipping. Jesus is here declaring His intent to accept this requirement ordained by YHWH to always and completely keep the Precepts of YHWH. Jesus is committing Himself to this extreme standard.

This is an extraordinary declaration and commitment, especially in light of the four-thousand-year track record of all other people. But if Jesus is going to fulfill all the requirements of righteousness, this is a commitment He will have to keep. And we cheer Him on because His success, followed afterwards by His exchanging with us His righteousness for our sin (Second Corinthians 5:21), is our only hope. He is committing Himself to accomplishing our righteousness for us! This is one of the recurrent themes of Psalm 119.

5. "Oh, that my ways were steadfast
   in obeying your decrees!" (NIV)

   Hebrew Literal: "O that   were established   my ways
   to keep   your statutes."

Meditations and commentary:

- This verse in the Hebrew is a little tricky to translate into English. The Hebrew word used in this verse and transliterated as "yikonu" can mean "may be ready" or "were established" or other such meanings as "were steadfast," as it appears in the NIV. I think of this verse as being translated into English in the following sense: "I am focused on making sure My ways are ready to keep Your Statutes." It is in this way that Jesus begins to express His intent and even longing for (the passionate embracing of) His commitment to consistently keep YHWH's decrees. He will continue to elaborate on this passion throughout this psalm.

6. "Then I would not be put to shame
   when I consider all your commands." (NIV)

   Hebrew Literal: "Then   not   do I would be ashamed
   when I look   unto   all   your commands."

Meditations and commentary:

- This concern Jesus has of not being put to shame occurs in four places in Psalm 119. It occurs here in v. 6, and vv. 31, 46, and 80. Jesus' concern about not being put to shame has little (or nothing) to do with His own personal embarrassment.

He is intensely concerned for the reputation of YHWH. Jesus is responsible for demonstrating that what God proposed to Adam and Eve was reasonable and desirable—specifically, that now this second Adam (Jesus; see 1 Corinthians 15:45) was here to demonstrate that relying on YHWH to make all decisions regarding what is good and what is not, and relying on His provision to lead us through those decisions, is a reasonable and desirable course of action, contrary to the one chosen by our first parents. Jesus was praying to ask YHWH to keep Him from bringing shame on the reputation of YHWH that would occur if Jesus failed to validate YHWH's original proposal to Adam. (Refer back to chapter two of this book for more discussion and background on this.)

7. "I will praise you with an upright heart
   as I learn your righteous laws." (NIV)

Hebrew Literal: "I will praise you   in uprightness   of heart
                  when I shall have learned   judgments   of your righteous."

Meditations and commentary:

- Here is a metaphor I hope will help with understanding this verse: A long time ago, when I was in the Army, I was once given the task of designing and building an obstacle course for a company of infantry trainees. It consisted of maybe about twenty different physical obstacles. I designed each obstacle and supervised a small group of soldiers as each obstacle was built. When we were done, we had a diverse set of obstacle events that were spread out across a distance of about a mile. I knew the obstacle course quite well. I was its designer. I was the one who saw to and supervised all the details of its construction. I had personally tested and approved each different obstacle event as it was built. The day came when we were done and the brigade commander (a very much senior and older officer than I was) wanted to experience our new obstacle course for himself. The course was designed to be run not by an individual, but by a two-man team. (Some of the obstacles required two people working together to properly complete.) The brigade commander chose me as his teammate. So, we ran the entire course together, for time, as it was designed to be run.

  Unknown to me before we started the course together, the brigade commander struggled daily with managing the minor, but sometimes painful, handicaps he endured from battle wounds he had received in the war. As we worked together to negotiate the various obstacles in the course, those handicaps and pain became evident. I remember feeling significant sorrow as I watched this older handicapped man put on a brave smile and endure the pain without ever a single complaint. But the entire experience made quite an impression on me. That experience was a new level of knowledge and understanding and insight about my obstacle course that I could not have known until I actually ran the course with that particular partner. So, even though I was the designer and builder of the course, some knowledge about the course could only be gained by experiencing it as a participant.

I think this metaphor is useful in helping me to grasp at least part of an understanding of how Jesus could be the designer and creator of the world and all its life, but at the same time, progressively increase in wisdom (Luke 2:52) as He experienced it as a participant the way it was designed to be experienced.

In the original plan of YHWH, rejected by Adam and now accepted by Christ, the Judgments/Laws of YHWH must be learned as life progresses. Not that the 613 Laws given by Moses couldn't be quickly memorized, but that their implications in the everyday details of an incarnate life become increasingly evident as that life unfolds through time. This progressive acquisition and experiencing of the application of those Laws and their corresponding insights into the person of YHWH, are a cause for great praise and rejoicing as they are revealed. Jesus did experience this progressive unfolding of revelation (see Luke 2:52), and He rejoiced greatly in it and praised YHWH for the ever unfolding experiential revelation of His glory.

8. "I will obey your decrees;
   do not utterly forsake me." (NIV)

   Hebrew Literal: "<u>Your statutes</u>   <u>I will keep</u>
   <u>not</u>   <u>do forsake me</u>   <u>utterly</u>   <u>very</u>."

Meditations and commentary:

- Someone said to me recently that Jesus was the most dependent person who ever lived. To give credibility to this statement he quoted John 5:30, "By myself I can do nothing; I judge only as I hear, and my judgment is just, for I seek not to please myself but Him who sent me." He also quoted part of John 8:28, "I do nothing on my own but speak just what the Father has taught me." And John 12:49, "For I did not speak on my own, but the Father who sent me commanded me to say all that I have spoken." (See also John 5:19 and Matthew 4:1-4, 11.)

Adam and Eve were convinced by Satan to figure it out on their own. Such a concept is anathema to Jesus. He <u>never</u> figured it out on His own. He was unflinchingly reliant on the provision of the Father for every decision He acted on and every word He spoke.

I think a useful paraphrase of this v. 8 is to see that Jesus is proclaiming, "I will keep your statutes, but I completely rely on Your help to do that." This underscores the distinct roles in the relationship between God the Father and God the Son that has been in operation from eternity before the world was created. This is the nature of the relationship God wanted to have with Adam and Eve, and this is the relationship that was so abhorrent to Satan.

Jesus was absolutely committed to living a life that was completely dependent on the spoken revelation of YHWH as written in the words of Scripture—and on YHWH continually guiding Him through the process of properly understanding and applying those words.

 Copyright © 2018, Richard L. Routh, All rights reserved.

Copyright © 2018, Richard L. Routh, All rights reserved.

ב **Beth (2)** – Theme: My joy comes from You leading Me according to Your word.

9. "How can a young man keep his way pure?
    By living according to your word." (NIV)

> Hebrew Literal: "<u>In what</u> <u>shall keep pure</u> <u>a young man</u>
>   <u>his way</u> <u>by keeping</u> <u>according to your word</u>."

Meditations and commentary:

- In Jesus' prayer to His Father in this verse, He is acknowledging the means by which He will keep His way pure. What does it mean to be pure?
    - Transparent (what you see is what you get)
    - No double motives and no hidden agenda
    - A heart that trusts His Father so much that there is no room at all for any type of distrust
    - Not embracing sin in any way (never doing what He might think is best unless it lines up perfectly with the Law of God)
    - Not envious of anyone or anything
    - Not adulterous or even lustful (see Matt 5:28)
    - Not falsely manipulative
    - And the list goes on and on

- Jesus lived according to the word of YHWH, which is to say, for <u>ALL</u> of His actions, Jesus only made choices that were in accordance to the word of YHWH.

- All of this, of course, is beyond us. We might dabble in being pure, but being pure cannot be a part-time endeavor. It is all or nothing. That is what pure means. So, we who are in Christ can rejoice that Jesus has accomplished this for us! Praise be to Jesus Christ, the only pure One!

10. "I seek you with all my heart;
    do not let me stray from your commands." (NIV)

> Hebrew Literal: "<u>With all</u> <u>my heart</u> <u>have I sought you</u>

<u>not</u>   <u>do let me wander</u>   <u>from your commands</u>."

Meditations and commentary:

- The rest of us might claim to wish we could seek YHWH will all our hearts, but only Jesus could actually do it. This is one of the many verses in Psalm 119 that could only ever have been truthfully prayed by Jesus Christ. Anyone else making this claim before the thrice Holy Lord God Almighty would be arrogant beyond belief and hopelessly delusional. Our blessing in all of this is that Jesus satisfied this requirement for us in our place. He did all the work, and we get all the benefit.

- If one is quickly and cursorily reading this verse, it might be easy to miss what I think is a surprising truth highlighted in this verse. Jesus is relying not on His own strength to keep the Commands of YHWH, but instead, He is expectantly relying on the provision of YHWH for that! This again underscores the eternal dynamic between God the Father and God the Son (the Father is the provider, and the Son is wholly dependent on Him for that provision), and it is a dynamic that Plan A from God had for us (but we rejected it in favor of us trying to be good in our own strength).

11. "I have hidden your word in my heart
    that I might not sin against you." (NIV)

Hebrew Literal: "<u>In my heart</u>   <u>have I hid</u>   <u>your spoken word</u>
                    <u>to the end that</u>   <u>not</u>   <u>do I might sin</u>   <u>against you</u>."

Meditations and commentary:

- What does it mean to hide God's word in our heart? For one thing, it means that Jesus' heart was set on seeking the satisfaction of His soul from the word of YHWH, as opposed to seeking to have his satisfaction come from worldly things such as a full stomach full of good food, or lots of money in the bank, or a well-funded 401-K plan, or great health insurance, or lots of status in the community, or the unconstrained ability to do whatever pleases His flesh, or a sense of purpose that comes from His accomplishments, or [you fill in the blank here].

- This verse raises the question: Do we sometimes sin because our heart is set on something other than the word of God? Or, is <u>THAT</u> the sin—that our heart is set on something other than the word of God? Maybe the behaviors and actions

 Copyright © 2018, Richard L. Routh, All rights reserved.

that we consider sinful are just the inevitable outward symptoms of wrong desires. If our heart is not constantly focused on storing up the word of God as though it were a treasure we were enthusiastically hiding away, then is THAT the sin? And all those wrong behaviors are only consequences of THAT sin?

- Maybe the reason Jesus never strays from the Commands of YHWH (see previous verse v. 10) is because He lets Himself desire ONLY the words of YHWH—which I think He sees as an inseparable manifestation from the Person of YHWH.

- If so, then is knowing God's word better a way to get to know God better? Is it possible this is intended by God to be the primary way to get to know Him better? If so, what are the ramifications of this truth on the application of John 17:3 in our lives?

- Does all this seem burdensome to you as you think about how hard it might be to change your thinking so that you always desire only to be satisfied by God's word? If so, then you are not yet connecting with a primary theme of this book. Although it is true that this is a requirement of righteousness from God, it is not a requirement for YOU! It is required only of Christ, who satisfied the requirement for you. So, what do we do now with all this stuff that was so crucially important to our Lord? If it was important to Jesus, shouldn't it be important to us if He is our Lord? Yes, of course it should. But the important thing to realize is that since Jesus has completely satisfied the full requirements of righteousness for us, we are no longer held responsible to do so. We are no longer judged or thought less of by God when we fail to walk as perfectly as Jesus walked (Romans 8:1). The pressure is off.

  We now have the privilege (as opposed to the responsibility) to dance in this new righteousness of the Law as Jesus danced in it; but now God is not criticizing us when we get a dance step wrong, or we get tired of dancing and want to take a rest, or in any other way we do it wrong. Jesus did it right, and His finished work is our claim before YHWH, not our efforts, or our heart, or our obedience, or whatever. So, just enjoy the dance and don't feel guilty if you get it wrong, because if you are in Christ, you are NOT guilty (so, why would it make sense for you to feel otherwise?). But in all this new freedom, do not forget that God is your friend and sin is not. As Paul says in Galatians 5:1, "It is for freedom that Christ has set us free. Stand firm, then, and do not let yourselves be burdened again by a yoke of slavery."

12. "Praise be to you, YHWH;
     teach me your decrees." (NIV)

Hebrew Literal: "Blessed are   you   YHWH
                        teach me   your statutes."

Meditations and commentary:

- If the decrees of God reflect His person and His character, and if God is infinite, then isn't it logical to expect that the full understanding of His decrees would require an infinite understanding? And if we have a finite mind, would it not stand to reason that it would be an overwhelming challenge for us to grapple with the proper understanding of His decrees for <u>any</u> given situation? The prayer Jesus is praying in this verse is a plea for YHWH to show Him the way, and then lead Him through this infinite puzzle. God has designed life so that "Normal" for us is NOT knowing what to do. "Normal" for us requires us to constantly rely on divine provision to lead us to the appropriate understanding (from His decrees) for every situation.

- This total and constant reliance on the leading and provision of YHWH is something that we are called to, and something that we should aspire to, but it is certainly something that we cannot do very well because we will not be very consistent in it. It is something Jesus has done perfectly. And praise be to Jesus, it is something Jesus has accomplished for those of us who are in Christ!

- If we want to know the mind and heart of Jesus, which is the purpose of this book, then we need to better understand and appreciate this dynamic of Jesus refusing to figure things out on His own, but instead, to continually rely on YHWH to give Him a proper understanding of how to apply the written Statutes of YHWH in every situation. To understand and appreciate this dynamic, we've got to **CHANGE THE WAY WE THINK ABOUT** righteousness. Specifically, we've got to NOT think about righteousness as something we accomplish, but instead, we must think about righteousness as something that God provides to us.

  This "RETHINKING" about how righteousness happens is at the heart of the Gospel. The Greek word "**<u>metanoia</u>**," which means to "**<u>change the way you think about</u>**," appears in the New Testament 56 times and it is often cited as a precondition for salvation. It is NOT a word that directly addresses our behaviors and actions. It is a word that asks us to change the focus of our attention.

  As a consequence of the Fall (see Genesis 3), our fallen nature is cut off from an intimate relationship with God in which God provides everything we need, and it confines us to experiencing reality only in the physical world. Our fallen nature compels us to figure everything out for ourselves. Our fallen nature requires us to want to <u>work</u> everything out for ourselves. Our fallen nature predisposes us to create some kind of system of "equitable exchange" whereby we trade our time, efforts and physical resources for outcomes that we want to see happen. This same fallen thinking (which the New Testament calls "carnal" or "fleshly" or "worldly" thinking) predisposes us to think about righteousness as something that we work for in accordance with some process of equitable exchange. In other words, it is the fallen thinking of our fallen nature that results in our assumption that righteousness is a result of our actions—a result of our "obedience" to the Law of God. This is an erroneous conclusion because it denies the fact that righteousness can only be provided to us by God. Jesus is the embodiment of our "new nature" which operates on the principle that God provides everything we need—including our righteousness. It is this new nature that we see in operation here in this verse when Jesus prays, "Teach me your Statutes."

At the risk of losing the focus on the flow of these verses in Psalm 119, please allow me to write a little more about the application in our lives of this very important insight. So, here is a corollary to what we have discussed above.

When we come to God in the habits of our fallen nature, we are predisposed by this belief in "equitable exchange" to think that we need to obey God so He will bless us, because then we will "deserve" His blessing. But, in reality, because YHWH, operating through Jesus, has already done all (completed) the work to make us righteous (and justified) in God's sight, our actions and behaviors are inconsequential (have no value) in making us more righteous (see Galatians 3-5). God does NOT see us as more righteous if we obey Him (versus disobeying Him). Jesus has provided us with ALL righteousness; it was His work, not ours.

Furthermore, if you are following this line of reasoning, I wouldn't even want God to take my "good" behaviors into account. I don't even want my actions to be brought to God's attention for His consideration—especially in determining what I deserve. I ONLY want Him to see Jesus' heart and actions. My "good" actions could only be an inferior distraction from Jesus' actions. To desire that God should take into account my "good" behaviors is a heartfelt repudiation of the sufficiency of the finished work of Christ. God is willing to give me what Jesus deserves, so why would I want to substitute that with what I deserve?

13. "With my lips I recount
all the laws that come from your mouth." (NIV)

Hebrew Literal: "<u>With my lips</u>   <u>have I declared</u>
<u>all</u>   <u>the judgments</u>   <u>of your mouth</u>."

Meditations and commentary:

- Why might Jesus have found it desirable (even necessary) to recount all the Laws that YHWH had spoken through Moses and the prophets? Let me answer that question with a question: If He (and we) were not focusing on the Laws (and holiness) of God, then what would He (or we) be focusing on?

14. "I rejoice in following your statutes
as one rejoices in great riches." (NIV)

Hebrew Literal: "<u>In the way</u>   <u>of your testimonies</u>   <u>I rejoice</u>
<u>as much</u>   <u>as in all</u>   <u>riches</u>."

Meditations and commentary:

- This a theme that recurs throughout this psalm and we will explore it in more detail later. But for now, let me say, "I praise you, Lord Jesus, that You rejoiced in following the Statutes of YHWH, and for You, those were Your "great riches!" I praise You that this was Your heart, and that it is now credited to me and my brothers and sisters!"

- And now, for us, the Lord Jesus Christ Himself is the "way" of YHWH's testimonies.

15. "I meditate on your precepts
and consider your ways." (NIV)

Hebrew Literal: "<u>On your precepts</u>   <u>I will meditate</u>
<u>and have respect</u>   <u>to your ways</u>."

Meditations and commentary:

- Lord Jesus, why were You meditating on YHWH's Precepts? What was the point? Since You are God, these were also Your Precepts, weren't they? So, why would You need to meditate on them?

- If You were "considering" His ways, then doesn't that mean You were either trying to discover new things about them, or at least, be reminded of them? Either way, it wasn't omniscience. It is clear that Your attitude was one of valuing the Precepts of YHWH and respecting His ways. Do I put Philippians 2:5-8 together with Luke 2:52 and conclude that Your incarnation meant that You were in a process, a gradual and continual arriving at a deeper understanding? Is this what it means that you grew (advanced) in wisdom?

- This is also a recurring theme throughout this psalm that we will explore in greater detail in later verses.

16. "I delight in your decrees;
I will not neglect your word." (NIV)

Hebrew Literal: "<u>In your statutes</u>   <u>I will delight myself</u>
<u>not</u>   <u>do do forget</u>   <u>your word</u>."

Meditations and commentary:

- Lord Jesus, it appears that the important thing for You was not what You knew, but what You treasured. Jesus, it is clear that You treasured and delighted in the word/Decrees of YHWH. It is clear that You were committed to not neglecting His word. Is it true that You saw His word and His Statutes as inseparable from the very Person of YHWH? When You were following His Statutes, was that You being intimate with the Father? Is that the way You want us to see the Statutes of YHWH?

- As we progress through the rest of this psalm, we will see that the answer to all three questions above is "yes."

Copyright © 2018, Richard L. Routh, All rights reserved.

ℷ Gimel (3) – Theme: Your Testimonies are My delight and My counselors and My refuge.

17. "Do good to your servant, and I will live;
   I will obey your word." (NIV)

> Hebrew Literal: "Deal bountifully   with   your servant
>   [that] I may live   and keep   your word."

Meditations and commentary:

- Vv. 17-20 should be read as a single unit so the theme is not missed.

- The "good" that is being asked for is "to open my eyes to see wonderful things in Your Law" (v. 18) so that He might know the truth for which He longs (v. 20) in contrast to all the strangeness (v. 19) that He finds around Him on this earth.

- Back in v. 12, He acknowledged that YHWH teaches Him about YHWH's Decrees. Hence, this flows into the next verse where Jesus prays, "Open my eyes that I may see wonderful things in your law."

- Jesus sees that YHWH's goodness comes to Him through YHWH's word, and that His (Jesus') life is defined by His keeping the Law of YHWH.

- Here is an ugly thought: Our sin nature predisposes us to see this verse as Jesus proposing a trade (a "fair exchange"). A very wrong and perverse interpretation of this verse would be to think that Jesus was saying, "If You do Your part and do good to Me, then I will do My part by obeying Your word." Such a thought would be abhorrent to Jesus. The fact is that Jesus already has an extreme desire to keep the word of YHWH. In this verse Jesus is asking YHWH to provide the life and insight so that Jesus will be able to continue keeping the word of YHWH.

- The way Jesus sees it, living a full and joyful life **IS** the same thing as keeping the word of His Father.

18. "Open my eyes that I may see
    wonderful things in your law." (NIV)

    Hebrew Literal: "<u>Open you</u>   <u>my eyes</u>
                      <u>and I may behold</u>   <u>wondrous things</u>   <u>from your law</u>."

Meditations and commentary:

- Jesus is praying for new insights into the wonders of God—insights that come from a better understanding of the Law of YHWH.

- This four verse set (vv. 17-20) culminates in a statement that only Christ can make: "My soul is consumed with longing for Your Laws at **ALL** times."

- Jesus is expecting that the wonders of YHWH that will be revealed to Him in the Law will completely satisfy His soul. This is the bread that Jesus spoke of in Matthew 4:4 and John 4:31-38. This implies that part of that requested revelation comes through the obedience of Jesus to the will of the Father (as expressed through His Commands). Jesus understood that the Father's role was to give Him understanding about the Law of YHWH. Even Jesus did not attempt to understand it on His own. As we will see in later verses, such an attempt would have been anathema to Jesus.

- Question: Do we approach the Law of God with the attitude and practice that it is our responsibility, and that by our efforts, we should dig out the guidance we seek from the word of God? (If you would answer "yes" to this question, or even if you wish you could answer "yes" to this question, then at least please see that Jesus sees a "yes" answer to be a very wrong approach to keeping the Laws of YHWH.)

19. "I am a stranger on earth;
    do not hide your commands from me." (NIV)

    Hebrew Literal: "<u>A sojourner</u>   <u>I am</u>   <u>on earth</u>
                   <u>not</u>   <u>do do hide</u>   <u>from me</u>   <u>your commands</u>."

Meditations and commentary:

- Those (everyone else—all the rest of us) who walk in the way of Satan's proposition to Adam and Eve (Genesis 3:1-7) pursue the satisfaction of their souls' needs in ways that are strange (and futile) to Jesus. He found no comfort and no satisfaction in the ways of fallen people who seek the satisfaction of their souls from their own efforts in the physical world.

- Jesus recognizes that unless YHWH reveals Himself through His Law (His Commands), He cannot be found.

- This is all not so much a picture of what we should do and how we should live, so much as it is a picture of what Christ has done and how He lived. His obedience is credited to us as righteousness (Second Corinthians 5:21). Our part is to trust that He has done this for us; our part is not to try to duplicate His work, but to allow Him to be our Sabbath rest and just rest in what He has accomplished for us (and provided to us). See Hebrews 4:9-11.

20. "My soul is consumed with longing
      for your laws at all times." (NIV)

Hebrew Literal: "Has broken   my soul   with longing
                  unto   your ordinances   at all   times."

Meditations and commentary:

- This is a remarkable statement that could only truthfully be made by Jesus Christ.   No one else could even come close to being able to make this claim.

- When we talk here about the needs of our souls, we are talking about such things as our need for purpose and significance, our need for hope, our need for joy, our need for freedom, our need for esteem, and our need for a sense of belonging. These are all needs of our souls. Jesus gets His soul's needs met exclusively by focusing only on the person of YHWH as He is revealed (as He reveals Himself) through His Law.

- We get our soul's needs legitimately met by letting Jesus do this for us—by looking unto Jesus as He gets His soul's needs met by the person of YHWH—as YHWH reveals Himself to Jesus through His Law.

- Please note: This opens the door for us to walk with Christ and to experience Him getting His soul's needs met by the revelation of YHWH in His Law. As we experience Jesus getting His soul's needs met, we share in those experiences which results in satisfying the needs of our souls.

21. "You rebuke the arrogant, who are cursed
and who stray from your commands." (NIV)

Hebrew Literal: "Have rebuked   the proud   [who are] cursed
who stray   from your commands."

Meditations and commentary:

- Vv. 21 and 22 should be viewed as a single compound sentence. It is one thought expressed from two different perspectives. It is important to recognize the logical dependence between these two verses because when one sees that the truth expressed in v. 21 establishes the context for the claim made in v. 22, it significantly amplifies the power of what is being prayed in v. 22.

- This verse (v. 21) states a truth that is expounded on throughout Scripture (Romans 3, Galatians 2:16, Galatians 5:4, Second Corinthians 3, etc.), which is: All of us are continually arrogant as we resort to our own strength and minds to attempt to accomplish good (as our first parents chose to do in Genesis 3:1-7), and the curse of God is on us because in doing so (which is our nature—our fallen nature), we arrogantly choose to pursue what we think is the best way to accomplish good instead of resting in the testimonies of God as they appear in His Commands. In this way, we stray from relying exclusively on the Commands of YHWH to show us what good looks like and to fully, with all our heart, trust God to implement in our lives the truths contained in His Commands. But Jesus NEVER made this mistake. Jesus always desired with all his heart to trust the leading of YHWH as YHWH revealed to Jesus the truths contained in YHWH's Commands, and as YHWH implemented those in Our Lord's daily walk—moment by moment, for ALL the moments in Jesus' incarnation. So, Jesus was never subject to the curse spoken about in this verse and therefore could make the claim and petition that appear in the next verse.

22. "Remove from me scorn and contempt,
for I keep your statutes." (NIV)

Hebrew Literal: "Remove   from me   reproach   and contempt
for   your testimonies   I have kept."

Meditations and commentary:

- In order for this book to make any sense to the reader, it is necessary to see and acknowledge that ONLY Jesus could make the claim that He kept all the Testimonies/Statutes in the way they were intended by YHWH to be kept.

- In order for the logical dependency between the first part and the second part of this verse to hold, it is logically necessary that the claim made in the second part ("for I kept your statutes") have no exception. In other words, for this verse to mean anything at all, it requires Jesus to be making the claim in the second part that He ALWAYS kept the Statutes of YHWH, without ever failing to do so.

- Jesus is making this claim before the Holy, Holy, Holy Lord, God Almighty, Who was, and Who is, and Who is to come: that Jesus deserves for YHWH to remove from Jesus scorn and contempt. He is making this claim on the basis of His own righteous merit!!! If one of us ever tried to do that, it would not end well for us, because it would be the height of arrogance on our part in that it would be a complete and bald-faced denial of our sin before the throne of the thrice-Holy God. That is a pretty scary thought. But for Jesus, it was a statement of fact and a reasonable basis for this plea.

- These two verses (vv. 21-22) should help the reader to see this is a messianic psalm that can only rightly be prayed in its full measure by Jesus.

- This verse also illustrates an example of the sort of thing Jesus prays on our behalf, because we cannot. See Hebrews 7:25 and Romans 8:34.

- But why was Jesus so concerned about scorn and contempt being directed at Him? Scorn and contempt are sometimes directed at me, and for the most part, I just ignore it. It's not a big deal for me. My internal response is to say to myself, "Consider the source," and then I take solace in remembering that Jesus is in charge of my reputation and it's not something I need to concern myself with. So, why was it such a big deal for Jesus? The reason this was a big deal for Jesus is that, because of Jesus' mission, role and identity, when people slandered Jesus, they were slandering YHWH. I suspect Jesus would not have much cared if people slandered Him, but the continuation of all of creation hangs on the reputation of the Holiness of YHWH. Because Jesus was the reflection on earth of the Father in heaven, then Jesus needed to have His own reputation protected so that His Father's reputation would be protected. Without it, all of creation would come unraveled. Remember, he taught us that when we pray, we should pray first (and foremost) for the name of the Father to be hallowed (Matthew 6:9).

23. "Though rulers sit together and slander me,
   your servant will meditate on your decrees." (NIV)

   Hebrew Literal: "Even though   did sit   princes   in   slander
                   against your servant
                   I will meditate   in your statutes."

Meditations and commentary:

- Regardless of the clamor of the false challenges to His reputation (see also v. 22) and all the negative fall-out that could entail, Jesus pledges Himself to not be distracted by all this noise, but to stay on mission. (In doing this, He is leaving this concern in the hands of YHWH.) His mission was, in part, to be the demonstration of the reasonableness of relying on the Statutes/Decrees of YHWH as the way to live an incarnate life. This was in contradiction to the proposition that Satan offered to Adam and Eve in Genesis 3:1-7. In so repudiating that proposition, Jesus lays the foundation for the healing and redemption of creation. So, not losing focus on keeping His life aligned with the Statutes/Decrees of YHWH is of primary concern. This is His focus and He cannot allow Himself to be distracted from it!

- Thank you, Lord Jesus, that you were not distracted by the concerns of the rich and powerful, but that you remained focused only on the Statutes of YHWH! I praise you for ignoring the agendas of the rich and powerful! (Which, by the way, means they are absolutely and permanently relegated to irrelevance. This fact establishes the basis of the objection and resistance the world has to Jesus Christ.)

24. "Your statutes are my delight;
   they are my counselors." (NIV)

   Hebrew Literal: "Also   your testimonies [are]   my delight
                   they are   my counselors."

Meditations and commentary:

- In this octet, there were multiple high points and low points—some examples of things in which Jesus greatly rejoiced, and some examples of threats and challenges He faced. The conclusion of the matters raised in this octet is expressed in this verse. When all was said and done, Jesus delighted in the Testimonies/Statutes of YHWH and embraced them as His trusted counselors. These Testimonies/Statutes of YHWH were His refuge and His strength!

- In contrast, if I by myself attempt to embrace the Statutes of God as given through Moses in the Scriptures (as opposed to letting Christ do this for me), then I find that they are not <u>my</u> delight. They are my enemy. They condemn me. They kill me. Except in Christ, I would run away from the Statutes of God. But Christ did not see the Statutes of YHWH as a challenge; He saw them as delightful and welcome counselors. This is something Jesus accomplished for me and my brothers and sisters. He was the Law keeper for us. He did for us what we cannot do for ourselves.

- I praise you, Lord Jesus, for You have kept the Law of YHWH for me!

ד Daleth (4) – Theme: You, YHWH, provide My deliverance in the path of your Commands.

25. "I am laid low in the dust;
    preserve my life according to your word." (NIV)

    Hebrew Literal: "<u>Cleaves</u>   <u>to the dust</u>   <u>my soul</u>
                        <u>revive me</u>   <u>according to your word</u>."

Meditations and commentary:

- As we begin to look at this fourth octet, it is helpful to recognize that the first four verses (vv. 25-28) need to be understood in the context of the troubles referred to in the last four verses (vv. 29-32). Specifically,
  - The deceitful ways of others (v. 29)
  - Non-truth (lies) (v. 30)
  - Shame (and mockery and tarnishing God's reputation) (v. 31)
  - Potential depression in response to the above (v. 32)

- The humility and vulnerability of Christ is on display in this octet. He was "laid low in the dust." The Lord of Glory was laid low in the dust. We know from later verses (vv. 81, 82, 83, 87) that He was pushed past His point of last strength (v. 81), past His point of understanding/knowledge/seeing (v. 82), past His point of last hope that things will get better for Him physically (v. 83), and nearly past His point of last endurance (v. 87).

- In this verse (v. 25) we see that Jesus seeks solution to these crises from the word of YHWH.

26. "I recounted my ways and you answered me;
    teach me your decrees." (NIV)

    Hebrew Literal: "<u>My ways</u>   <u>I have declared</u>   <u>and you heard</u>
                        <u>teach me</u>   <u>your statutes</u>."

Meditations and commentary:

- I think this is a dialogue between Jesus and His Father. Jesus is coming to the Father with an account of what He has done. This is in the context of being laid low in the dust.

- He receives affirmation from the Father; but Jesus wants to go further. He wants to see new ways to respond to the challenges of life and He knows those new insights will come from a better (deeper) understanding of the Decrees of YHWH, so He asks YHWH to teach Him from those Decrees. This attitude and activity of Christ is in conformance with the claim made about Him in Luke 2:52 that He "grew (advanced) in wisdom."

27. "Let me understand the teaching of your precepts;
    then I will meditate on your wonders." (NIV)

Hebrew Literal: "The way   of your precepts   make me to understand
                so shall I meditate   in your wonders."

Meditations and commentary:

- Jesus is looking for understanding that He does not yet have.

- He knows He can get this only from YHWH.

- His goal in His suffering—His desire in the midst of His suffering—His comfort in the midst of being laid low in the dust—is to be able to meditate on the wonders of YHWH. The meditation on the wonders of God is a gift of the highest order. It is a balm that effectively comforts, consoles, and strengthens us in the midst of our worst trials.

- YHWH! YHWH! YHWH! YHWH! YHWH! YHWH! YHWH! I walk boldly up to Your throne because I am in Christ!

28. "My soul is weary with sorrow;
    strengthen me according to your word." (NIV)

Hebrew Literal: "Melts   my soul   from grief

<u>strengthen me</u>   <u>according to your word</u>."

Meditations and commentary:

- Jesus' soul is pressed down and overburdened with sorrow.

- This sorrow comes from living in the midst of the deceitful ways of other men (v. 29). It comes from the lies that form the foundation of those deceitful ways—these lies which refute the Laws of YHWH (v. 30). It (sorrow) comes from the shame that comes from when others mock God's Law (Statutes). These are the things that cause Jesus to grieve and mourn. These are the things that melt the soul of the Son of God.

- He sees the remedy of this sorrow as, and His plea is for, the efficaciousness of YHWH's word—a comfort that even we who are disciples of Christ also experience.

29. "Keep me from deceitful ways;
    be gracious to me through your law." (NIV)

> Hebrew Literal: "<u>The way</u>   <u>of lying</u>   <u>remove</u>   <u>from me</u>
>   <u>and as to your law</u>   <u>be gracious</u>."

Meditations and commentary:

- This verse recognizes the dichotomy that, in the affairs of people, there are only two mutually exclusive kinds of things: God's Laws and people's lies. If something is not a Law of God, then it is a lie. That is a stark lens through which Jesus views reality.

- Jesus does not see the Law as a burden, but as the compassionate graciousness of a loving God. For Christ, the Law is a desirable gift, not something to be shunned. The Law puts us to death, but it gives life to Christ. We are unable and unwilling to keep the Law, but Jesus was both able and willing—and He kept the Law for us (in our stead)!

30. "I have chosen the way of truth;
I have set my heart on your laws." (NIV)

Hebrew Literal: "The way   of truth   I have chosen
your ordinances   have I set [before me]."

Meditations and commentary:

- Putting verses 29 & 30 together, Jesus sees the Laws of YHWH as the antidote for deceit and lies.

- He has set His heart on (His soul fully embraced) the Laws of YHWH.

- Jesus shows us here that we either revere and embrace the Law of God, or we accept and embrace deceit and lies. We do not have the option for some middle ground.

- We look for someone (anyone) who did fully desire and embrace the Law of God and we find Jesus, our King! Jesus validated the Law of God as a reasonable and desirable way to live life, and now that validation is on display for all to see. No longer can anyone reasonably claim that it is a preferable course of action for people to attempt to discern the distinction between good and evil apart from the revealed word of God.

31. "I hold fast to your statutes, YHWH;
do not let me be put to shame." (NIV)

Hebrew Literal: "I have stuck   to your testimonies   YHWH
put me not   do to shame."

Meditations and commentary:

- When we ask God to keep us from being put to shame, we ask on the basis of God's mercy and Christ's blood. But the Psalmist here is asking for God's deliverance on the basis of His own merits—on the basis of the fact that He has been consistent in His trusting in, and living according to, the Statutes of YHWH. This is an incredible claim, and one that only Christ could make.

- Jesus has held fast to the Statutes of YHWH for us. We can now claim the deliverance from shame based on the finished work of Christ.

- I praise You, Lord Jesus, because You have held fast to the Statutes of YHWH for me and my brothers and sisters.

32. "I run in the path of your commands,
for you have set my heart free." (NIV)

Hebrew Literal: "[In] the path   of your commands   I will run
for   you shall enlarge   my heart."

Meditations and commentary:

- Jesus finds the Commands of YHWH as something that sets Him free!

- The Commands of YHWH energize Him!

- Here we see the love Jesus has for the Commands of YHWH and that love exhilarates Him!

- He doesn't just walk in the path of YHWH's Commands, but He <u>runs</u> in them! Jesus gets pumped when He is faced with the Commands of YHWH; whereas, I get condemned and leveled (and rightly so, because I am a sinner!). Jesus was <u>not</u> a sinner.

ה **He (5)** – Theme: I (Jesus) long for and plead for You, YHWH, to accomplish Your work through Me.

33. "Teach me, YHWH, to follow your decrees;
     then I will keep them to the end." (NIV)

> Hebrew Literal: "<u>Teach me</u>   <u>YHWH</u>   <u>the way</u>   <u>of your statutes</u>
>   <u>and I shall keep it</u>   <u>[unto] the end</u>."

Meditations and commentary:

- Jesus is reveling (vv. 34-36, 40) in the fact that He needs the Father to teach Him (constantly teach Him) to follow His Decrees. The proper following of God's Decrees is not an obvious process for people. Even if there were no sin in our hearts, it would still be obscured, at least in part, by the fact that we have finite capabilities that are attempting to grasp infinite wisdom. The Statutes/Decrees of YHWH are infinite and can only be completely comprehended by the infinite YHWH, whose infinite character they reflect. Jesus not only recognizes, but revels in, the need for YHWH to teach Him the way through the proper implementation of these infinite Statutes in His finite incarnate life.

- When we think that being dependent on someone else, especially God, is not a good thing, we are being unwise at best, and most likely rebellious. The problem is that we focus on our own glory, apart from God. Here we see that Jesus is focusing not on His own capabilities, but on God's gracious provision. Jesus WANTS to be dependent on YHWH's goodness! It is an appropriate way for YHWH to be glorified in His (and our) life. After all, it is not about us, it is about God and His goodness. Why do we try so hard to minimize the goodness of God? Jesus didn't. He reveled in His dependency on the provision of YHWH as being a desirable and effective way to ensure that He (Jesus) would properly keep the Statutes of YHWH to the end.

- I have a friend who makes a big deal about the difference between the words "obey" and "keep." I mention it here because I think he has a valid point. "Obey" emphasizes our actions, and tends to focus us on behavioral outcomes. Whereas, "keep" tends to emphasize a heart attitude of consistent trust in the goodness and provision of God. If this distinction is an accurate assessment by my friend, then what is on display in this Psalm is not so much the behavioral outcomes of Jesus adhering to the letter of the Law, but instead it is the heart of Jesus yearning for the full acceptance of the gracious goodness of YHWH as provided for through His Law/Decrees/Statutes/Precepts/

34. "Give me understanding, and I will keep your law
and obey it with all my heart." (NIV)

> Hebrew Literal: "<u>Give me understanding</u>   <u>and I shall keep</u>   <u>your law</u>
>   <u>I shall observe it</u>   <u>with all</u>   <u>[my] heart</u>."

Meditations and commentary:

- In this octet, Jesus sees the Father's role as one of providing understanding (vv. 34-35), direction (v. 35), proper focus (vv. 36, 37), keeping promises (v. 38), public honor (v. 39), and preservation of life (v. 40); and Jesus sees His own role toward YHWH's provision as being to love it (v. 40), treasure it (v. 35), obey it (v. 34), rely on it (vv. 36, 37), witness to YHWH's goodness in it (vv. 38-39), and long for it (v. 40).

- This begs the question: What might it look like in our own lives if we were to imitate these roles and desires of Jesus toward the provision of God through His Law? Not to see the Law as a means to making us better Christians or more approved by God (because it certainly CANNOT do that), but to take on the same heart that Jesus had for the Source of provision of God's goodness in our lives?

35. "Direct me in the path of your commands,
for there I find delight." (NIV)

> Hebrew Literal: "<u>Make me to go</u>   <u>in the path</u>   <u>of your commands</u>
>   <u>for</u>   <u>therein</u>   <u>do I delight</u>."

Meditations and commentary:

- The difference in the NIV and the literal Hebrew for this verse is not a minor one. There is a big difference between God "directing" us, and God "making us to go." In the first case, the responsibility is on us, and in the second case God is not only the initiator but also provides for the implementation.

- I praise You, Lord Jesus, that You delight in the Commands of YHWH! Because now I and my brothers and sisters benefit from Your delight (because the Father now sees us as delighting in His Commands because we are in You)! And because of this, we are now free to delight in the Commands of YHWH.

- Lord Jesus, You are our King! You are the worthy One! You are the One Who has gone before us to clear the way of all obstacles to YHWH's approval and favor on us! (Because I was not, and will not on my own ever be, able to properly delight in the Commands of YHWH.)

- What is Jesus delighting in?
  - The directing/"making me to go" from YHWH?
  - The process of the path/journey?
  - YHWH's Commands?
  - All three?

- The structure of this verse puts the emphasis on "Make me go" which suggests Jesus is at least rejoicing in the relational roles, to wit, YHWH's role is to "make Jesus go" in the path of His Commands, and Jesus' role is to delight in that path and in those Commands and trust in YHWH's leading.

36. "Turn my heart toward your statutes
and not toward selfish gain." (NIV)

Hebrew Literal: "Incline my heart unto your testimonies
and not unto covetousness."

Meditations and commentary:

- Our fallen nature, resulting from and conforming to the proposition of Satan, is to have a tendency toward working to figure out how to maximize our own benefit. This focus and approach is opposite to that of a heart turned toward the Statutes of YHWH. Jesus has a heart turned toward the Statutes of YHWH. This is a heart that looks to YHWH for all its provisions, as opposed to working hard to provide for oneself.

- We either seek to increase our own glory or we seek to increase God's glory. (John 3:30)

- The desire of Jesus' heart is that His life should be preserved (vv. 37, 40), so that YHWH would be feared by people (v. 38), that people would see that God's Laws are GOOD and (v. 39), so that the righteousness that comes from the Precepts of

YHWH would be seen and known by all as the source of His life's preservation (v. 40).

37. "Turn my eyes away from worthless things;
    preserve my life according to your word." (NIV)

Hebrew Literal: "Turn away   my eyes   from looking at   vanity
        in your way   revive you me."

Meditations and commentary:

- Worthless things are those things that do not line up with the word of YHWH. They are either a lie, or their promise is a lie, or what they result in is the impoverishment of our souls.

- The word of YHWH is the actual truth; its promises come true and turn out to be more beautiful and desirable than they first appeared, and they result in the lasting enrichment of our souls.

- I praise You, YHWH, because Your word is a gift of Your goodness to us!

38. "Fulfill your promise to your servant,
    so that you may be feared." (NIV)

Hebrew Literal: "Establish   to your servant   your spoken word
        which [is]   to your fear."

Meditations and commentary:

- Jesus' concern for His own well-being is driven by His desire to see YHWH's reputation being feared among people. Something can be revered, but when it is mega-revered, it becomes intimidating. God is thrice holy and transcends time and space. That understanding of God should be so intimidating to us that we tremble in fear before His presence.

- Fearing God is a good and healthy and wholesome and life-giving thing.

39. "Take away the disgrace I dread,
for your laws are good." (NIV)

Hebrew Literal: "Turn away   my reproach   that   I fear
for   your judgments [are]   good."

Meditations and commentary:

- This seems to link the goodness of God's Laws with the removal of the threat of disgrace. The implication here is that the remedy or prevention of people thinking poorly of God is the elevation of the truth of His Laws.

- Specifically, it seems to suggest the following logic:
  - The goodness of YHWH's Law results in the removal of disgrace; therefore, we also see that:
  - Disgrace implies either that God's Laws are not good, or that we have not been aligned with God's Laws. Since Jesus was always aligned with God's Laws, disgrace was anathema to Him because it implied God's Laws were not good.

- Thinking about the quality and worth of God's holiness: God is extremely vested in upholding His reputation, and the reputation of those who are aligned with the Law of God. The highest alignment with the Law of God is to lean on the fact that Jesus kept the Law perfectly for us, which He did so that we would receive the full blessings of a Law Keeper. Praise be to God! This is part of the reason the book of Hebrews says that faith in Christ is better than the covenant from Moses.

40. "How I long for your precepts!
Preserve my life in your righteousness." (NIV)

Hebrew Literal: "Behold   I have longed   for your precepts
in your righteousness   revive me."

Meditations and commentary:

- Because we are in Christ, His life's preservation is our life's preservation. Jesus has kept the Law of YHWH for us!

- It is difficult (maybe, probably, impossible) to get this balance right. That is the balance of focusing on, and desiring first, YHWH and His righteousness, and then all else will follow. We want to focus on and desire the "all else" first. Praise be to God that Jesus has gotten this balance right and that He accomplished this for us!

 Copyright © 2018, Richard L. Routh, All rights reserved.

ו **WAW (6)** – Theme: I (Jesus) will boast of Your saving hesed, YHWH, that provides solutions according to the Judgments of Your word.

41. "May your unfailing love come to me, YHWH,
　　your salvation according to your promise." (NIV)

　　Hebrew Literal: "<u>Let come to me</u>　<u>your covenant loyalty (hesed)</u>　<u>YHWH</u> –
　　　　　　<u>[even] your salvation</u>　<u>according to your spoken word</u>."

AND

42. "Then I will answer the one who taunts me,
　　for I trust in your word." (NIV)

　　Hebrew Literal: "<u>and to answer him</u>　<u>reproaches</u>　<u>so shall I have [words]</u> –
　　　　　　<u>for</u>　<u>I trust</u>　<u>in your word</u>."

Meditations and commentary:

- These two verses (vv. 41 & 42) form a single sentence, so the commentary on them both is combined here.

- Jesus was/is God. What did He need to be saved from? Why would He ask His Father for salvation? Also, God's love is ALWAYS unfailing. Jesus knows that. Why would He pray (pleading) for those two things that are already a given? In His incarnate limited form, Jesus is illustrating several things, all of which are quite real and full of emotion for Him:

　- As humans, we are not designed to live, even for a moment, unconnected from the constant provision that flows to us from the life and person of YHWH.
　- Jesus was dealing with oppressive taunting. What was He being taunted about? Satan had a vested interest in Jesus failing in His mission to demonstrate the validity of the proposition that man should live in constant and complete reliance on the provision of YHWH for everything. This is a repudiation of the proposition Adam and Eve were offered by Satan in Genesis 3. If Jesus were to be successful in demonstrating the validity of relying on the goodness and provision of God for everything, then that would prove, once and for all, that the proposition of Satan

(that we should find it desirable to be the ones responsible for deciding what is good and what is not) would be proven to be fallacious—with the following consequence that all that Satan stands for, including our fallen nature, is invalid and can no longer be seen by anyone (people or angels) as a reasonable alternative; Satan's argument would be defanged and therefore Satan would be defeated. Therefore, God's proposition (as demonstrated in Genesis 1-2) would be validated.

- The oppressive taunting Jesus endured came in many forms, but one form certainly was demonstrated by His brothers in John 7:3-5, and is seen also Mark 3:21-22. Jesus was constantly being mocked and ridiculed for doing exactly what He was supposed to do; constantly doing only what He saw His Father doing (John 5:19). And that mocking often came from those who were closest to Him. If you are human (and Jesus is), then this mocking will bother you deeply. It bothered Jesus deeply because it damaged the fellowship bond He wanted to maintain with these people. So what did He do about this pain? He sought comfort and deliverance from His Father's word.

- The phrase in v. 42 "For I trust in your word" indicates the source of the ridicule He endured, as well as its solution. It was because Jesus constantly trusted in the word of YHWH, and exhorted others to do the same, that He was publicly (and privately) mocked as a "Mr. goody two-shoes."

- "For I trust in your word" also indicates the solution to this emotional oppression. Jesus found solace, encouragement, direction, and remedy in trusting the spoken revelation of YHWH as it appears in the Scriptures. He knows it to be eminently relevant and practically applicable to resolve the conflict in His soul that arises when He is oppressed by this sort of mockery.

- Every time we disregard the Law of God for our lives, we taunt Christ; but He has trusted in the word of YHWH for us.

- Jesus was (and is) a great lover of people. He enjoyed the comfort and encouragement and nourishment that came from quality fellowship, but when that fellowship turned on Him as a weapon, I suspect it was particularly grievous and burdensome to His soul.

43. "Do not snatch the word of truth from my mouth,
    for I have put my hope in your laws." (NIV)

Hebrew Literal: "<u>And not</u>   <u>do do take</u>   <u>out of my mouth</u>   <u>the word</u>

of truth   utterly   very –
for   in your judgments   I have hoped."

Meditations and commentary:

- Jesus was and is the Truth. His very Person defines truth for all of eternity. Why would He need to pray, "Do not snatch the word of truth from my mouth"? In His incarnate form, He was constantly reliant on the Father to give Him the key insights from the Laws of God that were appropriate for the moment. Jesus' hope came from this dynamic—that YHWH would reveal to Him, moment by moment, which Laws in what ways were to be applied in each situation. Even as a man, every time Jesus opened His mouth, it carried the full weight of Scripture. What an awesome responsibility!

44. "I will always obey your law,
   for ever and ever." (NIV)

   Hebrew Literal: "So I will keep   your law   continually
             forever   and ever."

Meditations and commentary:

- A commitment; a statement of fact; an imperative of reality; a divine promise!

- Should Jesus even only once fail to obey the Law of God, then all of reality, all of time, all of our future hope, would be undone. This is the responsibility that constantly rests on the shoulders of the Christ! And He has, and does, faithfully fulfill this commitment for us!!! Praise be to Jesus, the faithful one! Praise be to Jesus our King! Praise be to Jesus, the Law Keeper!

45. "I will walk about in freedom,
   for I have sought out your precepts." (NIV)

   Hebrew Literal: "And I will walk   in freedom –
             for   your precepts   I seek."

Meditations and commentary:

- In Jesus' view, seeking the Laws and Commandments and Precepts of God is the path to freedom. This thinking certainly runs counter to our fallen nature which sees any laws and commandments as a constraint—usually an unwelcomed constraint. God's Laws feel to our fallen human nature like a set of handcuffs that take away our freedom—even in the light of our own experiences that testify to us that our lives become less complicated when we follow the Laws of God! A metaphor of this phenomenon can be seen in our traffic laws. If everyone did not follow the laws that required drivers to stay in their assigned lanes and stop at red lights and stop signs, our roads would be places of carnage and destruction and we would be foolhardy to venture out into an environment where everyone did whatever they felt like. We would never know when that oncoming car would choose to come into our lane bringing death and destruction when it got to our car. We would be forced to creep along at much slower speeds and stop at every intersection to ensure our safety. Without traffic laws being rigidly obeyed by all drivers, our freedom to travel speedily and safely would be gone. Jesus saw this truth and rejoiced in the strict adherence to the precepts of God as a means to greater freedom in His everyday life. He continually sought greater understanding of how to apply the Precepts of God to each and every situation in His life—and as a result He walked about in great freedom.

  My own experience is that when I violate the Law of God, my soul fills with darkness. I am robbed of my peace. Instead of freedom, I get bondage. When I confess and turn from my disobedience, the darkness lifts, light fills my soul, and I am again free. I praise You Lord Jesus because You have won freedom for us through Your obedience!

46. "I will speak of your statutes before kings
and I will not be put to shame." (NIV)

Hebrew Literal: "<u>and I will speak</u>   <u>of your testimonies</u>   <u>also before</u>   <u>kings</u>
<u>and not</u>   <u>do be ashamed</u>."

Meditations and commentary:

- Those with great authority, who rule over the affairs of men, are continually cognizant of the impact the discharge of their responsibilities has on the lives of others. They do not quickly suffer fools; but they tend to be quick to recognize profundity. Their success depends on their access to profound counsel. It is to these powerful rulers that Jesus proudly presents the statutes of God as the profound secrets for which they are searching. Such was Jesus' respect, admiration and trust in the statutes of God.

47. "For I delight in your commands
because I love them." (NIV)

Hebrew Literal: "<u>And I will delight myself</u>   <u>in your commands</u>
<u>that</u>   <u>I have loved</u>."

Meditations and commentary:

- Love causes delight.

- In our fallen state, circumstances that are favorable to us in this physical world cause delight.

- But not with Jesus. His delight comes from His love for the Commands of YHWH, because they are <u>from</u> YHWH, and <u>that</u> causes Him to delight in those commands. His delight in the Laws of YHWH was a reflection of His delight in YHWH himself.

48. "I lift up my hands to your commands, which I love,
and I will meditate on your decrees." (NIV)

Hebrew Literal: "<u>also will I lift up</u>   <u>my hands</u>   <u>unto</u>   <u>your commands</u>
<u>that</u>   <u>I have loved</u>   <u>and I will meditate</u>   <u>in your statutes</u>."

Meditations and commentary:

- Work is generally done with our hands (prior to the information age).

- I think that the phrase "I lift up my hands" was a Hebrew colloquialism for "I begin to work on" or "I will do the work of" or "I will engage in the work of." It is a physical manifestation and symbol of the commitment of the will to "do it." In so doing, we show active devotion to the task we commit ourselves to work at.

- Jesus meditated on the decrees of God so
  - He would not lose focus on them
  - He would gain new insights into the person of YHWH
  - He would delight in the discovery of new applications of YHWH's Decrees.

- The major point here in these two verses (vv. 47-48) is that if you asked Jesus as He was walking along the dusty road from Galilee to Jerusalem, "Lord, what are You thinking about? What consumes Your constant focus? What delights Your heart more than anything else?" He would answer, "I constantly delight in the Commands of YHWH." And if you asked, "Why do You delight in the Commands of YHWH?" He would answer, "Because I love them." And then if you asked Him why He loves the Commands of YHWH, He would answer, "Because they teach Me about the will and heart of My Father. My Father delights in His Commands, because everything My Father speaks is truth, and they reveal His heart. My heart delights in His Commands because His heart delights in them, and I delight in Him and the things He delights in."

 Copyright © 2018, Richard L. Routh, All rights reserved.

ז **Zayin (7)** – Theme: I rejoice in My responsibility to keep Your Law, YHWH, for the benefit of My Church.

49. "[You do] Remember your word to your servant,
  For you have given me hope." (NIV)

   Hebrew Literal: "Remember   the word   to your servant
            on   that   you have caused me to hope."

   Meditations and commentary:

   - It is impossible to remind God of anything. He always has all things from all time in the center of His focus. If He didn't, they would cease to exist. So, Jesus is not reminding YHWH of His word/Promises to His servant. Jesus is comforting Himself with the reminder that YHWH never forgets a proclamation or promise or commitment He has made. He never even reconsiders them. As someone once said, "Has it ever occurred to you that nothing has ever occurred to God?"

   - Jesus' hope is in the proclamations of YHWH. There is nothing more rock solid and absolutely permanent than the proclamations of God. This is a source of great peace, comfort and hope for Jesus.

   - I praise you, Lord Jesus, that all your hope was in the promises of YHWH; because of that, now all our hope is in You!

50. "My comfort in my suffering is this:
  Your promise preserves my life." (NIV)

   Hebrew Literal: "This   [is] my comfort   in my affliction
            for   your spoken word   has revived me."

   Meditations and commentary:

   - I am sorry You had to suffer, Lord. I realize it might be true that You are not sorry about it and that You suffered willingly for me and my brothers and sisters because You love us. Maybe my regret is just an evidence of my fallen nature being at odds with the Divine Will, but the truth is that it causes me pain and indignation to see the Lord of glory suffering...even though I clearly see that You are at Your <u>most</u> glorious when You suffer to provide righteousness for me and my brothers and sisters.

- Thank You that You find comfort and strength and hope in the promises of the Father, even though those promises take You through the cross.

51. "The arrogant mock me without restraint,
    But I do not turn from your law. (NIV)

    Hebrew Literal: "<u>The proud</u> <u>have me in derision</u> <u>utterly</u> <u>very</u>
                          <u>from your law</u> <u>not</u> <u>do I did turn away</u>."

Meditations and commentary:

- Lord Jesus, an entire book, even an entire library, should be written, and no doubt will be written, about the extreme irony of the arrogant, mocking You about Your goodness and faithfulness. It is akin to Pilate asking in Your face, "What is truth?" while being oblivious to the fact that he was addressing the Quintessential Truth with that question.

- You were mocked for being so meticulously faithful to the Law of YHWH, but our hope is entirely predicated on Your perfect faithfulness to the Law of YHWH. Thank you that even when we were yet your enemies, You died for us!

- So, we were mocking You for saving us, and even so, You still saved us. That is because You, and not us, are the provider of our righteousness.

52. "I remember your ancient laws, YHWH,
    And I find comfort in them." (NIV)

    Hebrew Literal: "<u>I remembered</u> <u>your judgments</u> <u>from of old</u> <u>YHWH</u>
                          <u>and have comforted myself</u>."

Meditations and commentary:

- As His world (His fellowship associations) trembles and becomes unstable and fickle around Him, attacking His hope (v. 49), causing Him affliction to the point of threatening His life (v. 50), and society's mocking of Him because of His trust in the Law of YHWH, He finds solace and comfort in the fact that the Laws of YHWH are ancient and have stood the test of time. He takes refuge in the fact that the criticisms of the trustworthiness of God are not going to prevail; but the Law of YHWH will prevail.

53. "Indignation grips me because of the wicked,
who have forsaken your law." (NIV)

Hebrew Literal: "<u>Horror</u>   <u>has taken hold</u>   <u>of the wicked</u>
<u>who forsake</u>   <u>your law</u>."

Meditations and commentary:

- The forsaking of God's Law by the wicked is what makes Jesus <u>indignant</u>! From Jesus' perspective, the Law of YHWH is not optional. It is not just a smart thing to do. It is not just a wise thing to do. It is not just a nice thing to do. It is, in fact, an uncompromising moral imperative that brings the wrath of God when it is ignored. Lord have mercy on us!

- Praise be to Jesus Christ for keeping the Law of God for us! Because we certainly were not going to do it ourselves.

54. "Your decrees are the theme of my song
wherever I lodge." (NIV)

Hebrew Literal: "<u>Songs</u>   <u>have been</u>   <u>to me</u>   <u>your statutes</u>
<u>in the house</u>   <u>of my sojourning</u>."

Meditations and commentary:

- Jesus's attitude toward the Decrees of YHWH was not one so much of dutifully obeying moral constraints; His attitude was more one of celebration and rejoicing in the Decrees of YHWH. The Decrees of YHWH were the music of His soul. He found them precious, endearing, and they inspired and encouraged His heart.

- "In the house of my sojourning"—A poetic metaphor for being in His incarnate body; and a personal reminder of His mission that required Him to have an incarnate body.

- Praise be to You, Lord Jesus, for having the right attitude toward the Decrees of YHWH! This is one more thing You accomplished for me and my brothers and sisters!

55. "In the night I remember your name, YHWH,
    and I will keep your law." (NIV)

Hebrew Literal: "I have remembered   in the night   your name   YHWH
                    and have kept   your law."

Meditations and commentary:

- "In the night" –was this a poetic metaphor for the dark times of the soul?

- At least it was that Jesus dreamed about remembering the name of YHWH and keeping His Law. This goes along with His proclamation in v. 54 about the Decrees of YHWH being the theme of His song.

- Also, what is so heavy on your heart that it keeps you up at night? For Jesus, it was the reputation of YHWH as displayed by His (Jesus) faithful following of the Laws of YHWH (see v. 62).

56. "This has been my practice:
    I obey your precepts." (NIV)

Hebrew Literal: "This   has fallen   to me
                    because   your precepts   I kept."

Meditations and commentary:

- Lord Jesus I praise You that it has been Your responsibility and Your consistent and faithful practice to keep the Precepts of YHWH, and that You kept them for me and my brothers and sisters. Surely, You have provided righteousness for us!

ח **Heth (8)** – Theme: I (Jesus) am committed to demonstrating that Your mercies, YHWH, come through Your Statutes.

57. "You are my portion, YHWH;
      I have promised to obey your words." (NIV)

     Hebrew Literal: "[You are] my portion   YHWH
                      I have promised   to keep   your words."

     Meditations and commentary:

     - Can anyone other than Jesus Christ make and keep this promise?

     - In Luke 6:46, Jesus asks, "Why do you call me, 'Lord, Lord,' and do not do what I say?" That was <u>not</u> a mistake that Jesus made in His relationship with His Father (YHWH).

     - I praise You, Lord Jesus, that You were consistently obedient to the words of YHWH for me and my brothers and sisters.

     Question for you: Can anyone other than Jesus keep a promise to always obey the word of YHWH?
     (Please write out your best answer to this question in the space provided below. Thank you!)

58. "I have sought your face with all my heart;
      be gracious to me according to your promise." (NIV)

     Hebrew Literal: "I entreated   your favor   with all   [my] heart
                      be merciful to me   according to your spoken word."

     Meditations and commentary:

     - We are reliant on the grace of God because we have no merit of our own–we have done nothing that enables us to claim access to His presence; our access to His presence is entirely earned for us by the finished work of Christ. But the deficit that is so glaring in me is not a deficit that exists in Jesus. Jesus can approach YHWH on the basis of His own merit. (That is why He can be our high priest.) So, why is Jesus asking for YHWH to be gracious/merciful to Him?

Jesus is asking for YHWH to be gracious to Him because YHWH is infinite and we (including the incarnate Christ) are finite. The finite cannot comprehend the infinite unless the infinite gives that revelation to the finite in such a way that it is appropriate for the moment. That is what Jesus is asking for. It is the prayer of the finite asking for the truth of John 17:3 to be fulfilled in his life. That fulfillment must be (can be) provided only by the Father (YHWH).

Question for you: In your own words, please explain the main point being made by Jesus in John 17:3.

(Reminder: Please write out your best answer to this question in the space provided below. Thank you!)

59. "I have considered my ways
and have turned my steps to your statutes." (NIV)

Hebrew Literal: "I thought   on my ways
and turned   my feet   unto   your testimonies."

Meditations and commentary:

- Introspection is a necessary aspect of healthy accountability—an accountability that results in mid-course corrections when appropriate.

- It is an accountability for the purpose of ensuring that His steps were aligned with the Statutes of YHWH.

- A possible alternative translation of the Hebrew is: "YHWH, My portion is the promise I have made to keep Your words." This rendering certainly rings with the echoes of the halls of eternity.

- This concern and commitment is consistent with sentiments expressed in v. 57 (promise to obey), v. 58 (seeking with all His heart), and v. 60.

- When you find yourself questioning whether you are going the right way in some area or activity of your life, then you might want to remember two things:

    1. This was a common practice of Jesus, and

    2. He found the direction and confirmation He sought in the Testimonies/Statutes of God's word.

Question for you: When Jesus said, "I thought on my ways" (see the Hebrew Literal), what kind of things specifically do you think He was thinking about?

(Reminder: Please write out your best answer to this question in the space provided below. Thank you!)

60. "I will hasten and not delay
     to obey your commands." (NIV)

     Hebrew Literal: "<u>I made haste</u>   <u>and not</u>   <u>do delayed</u>
                     <u>to keep</u>   <u>your commands</u>."

     Meditations and commentary:

     - Jesus is not interested in, or inclined to, stall in His obedience. Instead, He is in an enthusiastic hurry to obey the commands of YHWH.

     - It seems to me based on several such verses throughout Psalm 119, that Jesus is genuinely hungry to get as deeply engrossed with as many of the Laws, Commands, Statutes, Decrees and Precepts of YHWH as He possibly can. This is His oxygen and the more He gets, the faster and farther He can run! The more engrossed in the Commands of God He can get, the more enjoyment in life He will have!

     - I praise You, Lord Jesus, for taking away the burden of the Law for us, and replacing it with the joy **You** have for the Law!

     Question for you: What is the "oxygen" of your life? What causes you to become more enthusiastically engaged in life?

61. "Though the wicked bind me with ropes,
     I will not forget your law." (NIV)

     Hebrew Literal: "<u>The bands</u>   <u>of the wicked</u>   <u>have encircled me</u>
                     <u>your law</u>   <u>not</u>   <u>do have I forgotten</u>."

     Meditations and commentary:

- This is prophetic because Jesus was bound with ropes by the wicked, and tortured, as a prelude to His crucifixion. Yet, even in the midst of this persecution and pain, His commitment to the Law of YHWH did not waver.

Question for you: When Jesus says here "the bands of the wicked have encircled me" (see the Hebrew Literal), if the word "bands" is not intended to be literal ropes, then metaphorically what else might these "bands" be?

62. "At midnight I rise to give you thanks
     for your righteous laws." (NIV)

     Hebrew Literal: "At mid-   night   I will rise   to give thanks   to you
                     because of   judgments   your righteous."

     Meditations and commentary:

- Jesus rejoiced in the righteousness of God's Laws. There is even something in us that rejoices in that righteousness. This is why we like movies where the good guy wins in the end and the bad guy is punished. Even in our fallen state, we still rejoice when things turn out right. Jesus had/has this same kind of rejoicing in the righteousness in the Laws of YHWH.

     Question for you: When you think about the Ten Commandments, are there any of those ten that make you think, "Wow! I sure am glad God has committed Himself to enforcing that one among humans!" ?

63. "I am a friend to all who fear you,
     to all who follow your precepts" (NIV)

     Hebrew Literal: "A companion   I am   of all   those who   fear
                     you and of those who keep   your precepts."

     Meditations and commentary:

- In John 15:15, Jesus defines a friend as someone who He confides in by making known to them everything He learned from the Father. He contrasts "friend" with "servant" because a servant is "not in the know" about his master's business.

- Putting v. 63 together with John 15:15, gives us the sense that Jesus confides in all those who fear God; and that His closest confidences are His understandings of how to better follow the Precepts of God. The point here is that Jesus regards the understanding about the Precepts of God as precious secrets only to be shared with His friends.

- Do you want to be one of Jesus' friends? Are you interested in having Him share with you His precious insights into the Precepts of God as they are written in the Scriptures?

Question for you: Here the N.I.V. translates the Hebrew word for "keep" to be the English word "follow." In most places in this psalm, the N.I.V. translates the Hebrew word "keep" to be the English word "obey." Is there a difference between "keeping" and "obeying"? If so, what do you think that difference might be?

64. "The earth is filled with your love, YHWH; teach me your decrees." (NIV)

Hebrew Literal: "Of your covenant loyalty   YHWH   is full   the earth your statutes   teach me."

Meditations and commentary:

- "Teach me your decrees" or "your statutes teach me"? Jesus is not so much asking to have the Decrees of YHWH recited to Him as He is rejoicing in how the Statutes of YHWH teach Him about the kindness and faithfulness of YHWH as it is displayed in the earth. (The Law of Gravity would be an example of the kindness and faithfulness of YHWH displayed in the world around us.)

- Furthermore, the focus here is on the love of YHWH and how it pervades everything there is. Jesus sees the Decrees of YHWH as being testimonies of the love of YHWH and He is rejoicing in the connection between the love of YHWH and the Decrees of YHWH.

Question for you: Have you ever thought of the Laws of Physics and Mathematics as being corollaries of the Laws of Moses?

ט Teth (9) – Theme: Affliction helps Me keep your Law, YHWH, which results in great benefit for me.

65.   "Do good to your servant
          according to your word, YHWH." (NIV)

      Hebrew Literal: "Well   you have dealt   with   your servant
                         YHWH   according to your word."

      Meditations and commentary:

      • That Jesus would need to pray for YHWH to do good to Him is perplexing. Was this just a recognition of YHWH's goodness to Him? Was it necessary to ask? (v. 68—"what You do is good") Did this move the Father to treat the Son better?

      • Looking at the Hebrew Literal for this verse, one gets the sense that this is more a praise of gratitude to YHWH for the goodness of His word as the means for providing abundantly for Jesus' needs.

      Question for you: Would it be good for us to view the word of YHWH in this way? We who are in Christ do view the Word of YHWH (Jesus) in this way, but would it also be good for us to view the word of YHWH (the spoken words of YHWH that comprise the Scriptures) in this way, as Jesus did?
      (Reminder: Please write out your best answer to this question in the space provided below. Thank you!)

66.   "Teach me knowledge and good judgment,
          for I believe in your commands." (NIV)

      Hebrew Literal: "Good   judgment   and knowledge   teach me
                         for   in your commands   I have believed."

      Meditations and commentary:

      • The justification for YHWH to teach Jesus knowledge and good judgment (see Luke 2:52) was that Jesus trusted in YHWH's Commands. This is a remarkable declaration of the way in which YHWH responds to those who trust in His

Commands.

- How would our lives be different if we trusted YHWH to be faithful to us in accordance with the promises (explicit and implicit) contained in His Commands?

- When we trust Christ to be our savior, we **are** trusting that those promises come to us because of Christ's trust in them!

Question for you: How would your life be different if you trusted YHWH to be faithful to you in accordance with the promises (explicit and implicit) contained in His Commands?

67. "Before I was afflicted I went astray,
 but now I obey your word." (NIV)

Hebrew Literal: "<u>Before</u>   <u>was afflicted</u>   <u>I [am]</u>   <u>I went astray</u>
 <u>but now</u>   <u>your spoken word</u>   <u>have I kept</u>."

Meditations and commentary:

- For Jesus: ignorance implies going astray (non-optimal judgments), which further implies affliction, which further implies the need to get more knowledge (of a more optimal way), which is supposed to result in better judgment about why, what, and how we do things. The fact that Jesus "grew (advanced) in wisdom" (Luke 2:52) is the explanation of this verse. Not knowing everything is NOT a sin, but not knowing everything causes us to act in non-optimal ways. In other words, to act in not the wisest way.

- Does obeying God's word decrease our affliction? Or does it just bring affliction at a higher level of wisdom?

- Affliction: we are conformed to His image through the fellowship of His suffering.

- How can a good God let this affliction happen? Because He is loving and takes a longer view, He has blessed me with this affliction. I can trust in God's goodness because Jesus did.

Question for you: If God the Father loved Jesus, why would He let Jesus be afflicted?

68. "You are good, and what you do is good;
   teach me your decrees." (NIV)

   Hebrew Literal: "<u>Good   yourself   and do good</u>
                  <u>teach me   your statutes</u>."

   Meditations and commentary:

   - By learning the Decrees of YHWH, we study His goodness. If we want to know more of the goodness of God, we need to study His Decrees. This is part of how Jesus sought the face of YHWH.

   - The full understanding of YHWH's Decrees is not explicitly obvious in the written Law, but the Decrees of God need to be ferreted out from what <u>is</u> written. YHWH must lead us in this—He must teach us what He intends. This was how Jesus saw it.

   Question for you: Can you list 5 good things we discover about the Person of God by studying His Decrees/Statutes?

69. "Though the arrogant have smeared me with lies,
   I keep your precepts with all my heart." (NIV)

   Hebrew Literal: "<u>Have forged   against me   a lie   the proud</u>
                  <u>I [am]   with all   [my] heart   will keep   your precepts</u>."

   Meditations and commentary:

   - This is one of many statements in Psalm 119 that only Jesus could make. Anyone else making this statement is being arrogant or presumptuous or blind to sin. What other verses in Psalm 119 are evidences that only Jesus Christ, in all of history, could have truthfully prayed this psalm?
     - **v. 69:** Though the arrogant have smeared me with lies, I keep your precepts with all my heart.

- **v. 57:** You are my portion, O Lord ; I have promised to obey your words.
- **v. 51:** The arrogant mock me without restraint, but I do not turn from your law
- **v. 22:** Remove from me scorn and contempt, for I keep your statutes.
- **v. 20:** My soul is consumed with longing for your laws at all times.
- **v. 3:** They do nothing wrong; they walk in his ways.
- **v. 106:** I have taken an oath and confirmed it, that I will follow your righteous laws.
- **v. 31:** I hold fast to your statutes, O Lord ; do not let me be put to shame.
- **v. 121:** I have done what is righteous and just; do not leave me to my oppressors.
- **v. 129:** Your statutes are wonderful; therefore I obey them.
- **v. 131:** I open my mouth and pant, longing for your commands.
- **v. 153:** Look upon my suffering and deliver me, for I have not forgotten your law.
- **v. 173:** May your hand be ready to help me, for I have chosen your precepts.
- **v. 174:** I long for your salvation, O Lord , and your law is my delight.
- **v. 34:** Give me understanding, and I will keep your law and obey it with all my heart.

- What are these lies that the arrogant have smeared Jesus with?
    - "He is a Law breaker."
    - "He is of Satan."
    - "He is crazy."
    - "He is a blasphemer."
    - "He seeks His own glory."
    - "He came to abolish the Law."
    - "He lies."
    - "He arrogantly assumes an authority He is not worthy of."
    - "He falsely claimed that God would rescue Him."

- But here is the truth: "I keep Your Precepts with all My Heart."

Question for you: What is it about Jesus that makes the proud want to accuse Him?

70. "Their hearts are callous and unfeeling,
    but I delight in your law." (NIV)

Hebrew Literal: "Is covered   with fat   their heart
                 [but] I   in your law   delight."

Meditations and commentary:

- This verse is a continuation of the previous verse, so the "their" in this verse refers to "the proud" in v. 69.

- Lord, I praise You that You delight in the Law because You did that for me and my brothers and sisters! God now credits us with always delighting in the Law!

- I praise You Lord Jesus because You have accomplished righteousness for me and my brothers and sisters.

Question for you: How are being "proud" and not delighting in the Law of God connected? Does "not delighting" in God's Law cause one to be proud, or does being proud cause one to not delight in God's Law, or is it both?

71. "It was good for me to be afflicted
        so that I might learn your decrees." (NIV)

    Hebrew Literal: "[It is] good   for me   that   I been afflicted
                      to the end that   I might learn   your statutes."

Meditations and commentary:

- This is further elaboration on the thought expressed in v. 67, and confirmation of the thoughts that appear in its commentary.

- 2 Timothy 3:16: "All scripture is God-breathed and is useful for:
    - teaching
    - rebuking
    - correcting
    - training in righteousness

    so that the man of God may be thoroughly equipped for every good work."

Question for you: Is affliction necessary if we are to learn the Statutes of God? Why? How does affliction relate to growing in wisdom?

72. "The law from your mouth is more precious to me
    than thousands of pieces of silver and gold." (NIV)

Hebrew Literal: "[is] better   to me   the law   of your mouth
                    than thousands   of gold   and silver."

Meditations and commentary:

- This is strong evidence of Jesus' kingship and nobility. His priority, passion and sense of reality are focused on the testimonies of YHWH. This is what makes Jesus different. This is a point of divine leadership. The heart of Christ calls me and my brothers and sisters to value the testimonies and trustworthiness of God over any of the solutions that could possibly come from this physical world (even on its best day).

- More commentary on this verse appears in the commentary for v. 127.

Question for you: Would you be willing to trade $100 million dollars in lottery winnings for a better understanding of the Law of God?

(Please note: If your answer to the above question is "yes," then this book is **_way_** underpriced! ☺)

ʾ **Yodh (10)** – Theme: YHWH's compassion is to teach Me His Commands, which give me comfort, hope, and cause others to follow Me.

73. "Your hands made me and formed me;
      give me understanding to learn your commands." (NIV)

     Hebrew Literal: "<u>Your hands</u>   <u>have made me</u>   <u>and fashioned me</u>
                           <u>give me understanding</u>   <u>and I may learn</u>   <u>your commands</u>."

Meditations and commentary:

- This is a plea for YHWH to finish what He has started. Jesus is acknowledging that YHWH knows how His creation works. YHWH knows how to give us understanding to learn His Commands, because He created us.

- Jesus wants to better understand how to learn more about the Commands of YHWH. It is not just memorizing the 613 explicit Commands/Laws that were written by Moses, but it is a matter of gaining deeper insights about how and when to best apply them.

- An example of where these deeper insights show up in the New Testament (there are many) is in the Sermon on the Mount (Matthew 5-7). Jesus points out that the hearer of the law might only have heard and understood that we should not murder other people, but did we also see that the deeper meaning of this command to not murder is an injunction to not hate and to not speak disparagingly about others?

  And again, Jesus points out that the hearer of the Law might have only heard that we should not commit adultery, but did we also see the deeper meaning of this command was to not lust or think in a debasing way about others?

  And again, Jesus wants us to see that the Command to not steal is really pointing us to a deeper realization that we should not put our heart into storing up treasures on earth where they will decay and be destroyed, but instead we should put our heart into the treasures we have in heaven which cannot be lost. By the way: When Jesus is talking about the treasures we have in heaven, He is talking about treasures we have <u>NOW</u> in heaven. These are heavenly treasures that we are to enjoy in this present time. He is not talking about treasures that we will receive at some future time after we die (except for the consequence that we will <u>still</u> have them after we die because they are not diminished by the events of time). If the reader is intrigued by this line of thought, then please take a look at Psalm 73:25-28, which will provide better definition of this heavenly treasure and how we are enriched by it now, in this life. This also is an elaboration on John 17:3, which is what life is all about.

Question for you: What is the reason the incarnate Jesus gives in this verse for why YHWH should give Him understanding to learn His Commands?

(Reminder: Please write out your best answer to these questions in the space provided below. Thank you!)

74. "May those who fear you rejoice when they see me,
      for I have put my hope in your word." (NIV)

Hebrew Literal: "May those who fear you   when they see   also be glad in me
                  because   in your word   I have hoped."

Meditations and commentary:

- I praise You Lord Jesus that You get Your hope from the word of YHWH. You have done this for me and my brothers and sisters; so, our hope is now in the word of YHWH (even if we don't recognize that it is).

- I am not sure there is a truer statement than "those who fear YHWH rejoice when they see Jesus!!!" This petition of Christ's has certainly been answered by His Father! Jesus is the absolute source of all of our rejoicing! As a matter of fact, what else is there for us to rejoice in?

Question for you: We all need hope. Without it humans quickly die. Where did Jesus get hope from?

75. "I know, YHWH, that your laws are righteous,
      and in faithfulness you have afflicted me." (NIV)

Hebrew Literal: "I know   YHWH   that [are]   right   your judgments
                  and in faithfulness   you have afflicted me."

Meditations and commentary:

- See this in the context of verses 67 and 71 in the previous octet (Teth). Affliction from God is a loving, gracious gift that corrects our path to be better aligned with the righteous Laws of YHWH. Since our lives are most fulfilled when our thinking and our hearts and our actions are right, then the most loving, gracious thing God can do for us is to get us better aligned with the goodness of His righteous Laws.

- Jesus knew all this and that is why He asks for, even rejoices in, affliction from YHWH—it is because in God's faithfulness to us, He corrects and trains us to know Him better through conformance with His character, which is discovered and experienced as the incarnate Christ becomes more deeply aligned with the Laws of YHWH (remember Luke 2: 52, "Jesus <u>grew</u> (advanced) in wisdom").

- Praise be to Jesus for being obedient for us!

- Praise be to Jesus for desiring conformance to God's Laws more than He desired to avoid affliction—and this righteous desire is to our credit! He has accomplished this for us! He did the work, and now we get the credit for His accomplishments, as well as the ensuing benefits (Second Corinthians 5:21).

Question for you: For you, what are some of the "ensuing benefits" that you get from Jesus' accomplishments?

76. "May your unfailing love be my comfort,
  according to your promise to your servant." (NIV)

Hebrew Literal: "<u>May be</u> <u>I pray</u> <u>your merciful covenant loyalty</u>
          <u>for my comfort</u>
          <u>according to your spoken word</u> <u>to your servant.</u>"

Meditations and commentary:

- Putting this verse into the broader context of this octet and of all of Psalm 119, Jesus is acknowledging that YHWH's <u>unfailing love</u> is expressed in His Laws and Commands and Precepts. His Laws are not harsh constraints; they are the loving provisions that come from the heart (promise) of YHWH, and as such, they bring great comfort to Jesus.

- Jesus sees that the Laws of YHWH are expressions (and provisions) of the <u>rock-solid</u> faithfulness of YHWH according to His promise. That stability and certainty gives Jesus comfort.

- Do we regularly go to the word of God for the comfort of our soul?

Question for you: Do you regularly go to the word of God for the comfort of your soul?

77. "Let your compassion come to me that I may live,
    for your law is my delight." (NIV)

Hebrew Literal: "Let come to me   your tender mercies   and I may live
      for   your law   [is] my delight."

Meditations and commentary:

- Jesus delighted in the fact that the tender mercies of YHWH come to Him through the Law of YHWH. Jesus saw that delight for the Law of YHWH opens the door to better understanding the compassions of YHWH; and that the compassion of YHWH is salvific.

- One could hardly dare to make a claim to the saving compassion of YHWH based on ones delight in the Law of YHWH, unless that One had unfailingly and unceasingly delighted in His Law. Even this has been accomplished for us by Christ!

- Whatever Jesus did, whatever Jesus desired in His heart, whatever Jesus regarded as valuable, whatever Jesus truly loved: we get the credit and benefit for it all because of Second Corinthians 5:21.

Question for you: Do you see the Law of God as a vehicle by which you are brought the tender mercies of God?

78. "May the arrogant be put to shame for wronging me without cause;
    but I will meditate on your precepts." (NIV)

Hebrew Literal: "Let be ashamed   the proud   for   outside a cause
      they dealt perversely with me

<u>[but] I</u>   <u>will meditate</u>   <u>on your precepts</u>."

Meditations and commentary:

- The claim of the arrogant is the result of Adam and Eve accepting Satan's proposition (Genesis 3: 1-7). Satan's proposition is that we should be given the right to decide what is good and what is not good. This claim is the height of arrogance because it elevates us while debasing God. Jesus is asking that those who think they have a right to "decide what is fair" be publicly shown to be fools (which is what they are).

- Instead, Jesus chooses to ignore the "right to decide what is fair" in favor of trusting in the Precepts of YHWH. He is proclaiming His commitment to focus on how to understand and apply the Precepts of YHWH. This is in direct opposition to those who have taken up the right to decide for themselves what they should do and how they should do it.

   Question for you: What remedy is recommended by this verse for when you are falsely accused? How would that work in your life?

79.   "May those who fear you turn to me,
      those who understand your statutes." (NIV)

   Hebrew Literal: "<u>May turn</u>   <u>to me</u>   <u>those who fear you</u>
                   <u>even that they may know</u>   <u>your testimonies</u>."

Meditations and commentary:

- Notice the difference between the NIV and the Hebrew Literal. What if Jesus is praying: "May those who fear You turn to Me, so that in doing so, they may experientially know and truly understand the real point of Your Testimonies." If so, then Jesus is praying here for our salvation. In the midst of being afflicted (v. 75) and mocked (v. 78), Jesus is claiming the promise made to Him by the Father (v. 76) that all this suffering will result in our salvation. He was delighted (v. 77) to suffer because in this way He would provide us with changed hearts that would know by faith that Jesus is the Keeper of the Law and that He did it for us. Why? So that all righteousness would be accomplished through Him by The Father and provided to us.

- Jesus desires to share with us (those who fear YHWH) His love for, and devotion to, and the benefits that come from, the Statutes of YHWH. The greatest of these benefits is getting to better experientially know the heart and mind of God. (John 17:3 and Psalm 73:25)

Question for you: Has it ever occurred to you that the greatest treasure you could get out of this life is the depth of the knowledge and relationship you have with God The Father and His Son, Jesus? (See John 17:3)

80. "May my heart be blameless toward your decrees,
    that I may not be put to shame." (NIV)

Hebrew Literal: "Let be   my heart   sound   in your statutes
                to the end that   not   do I will be ashamed."

Meditations and commentary:

- "May my heart be kept blameless (Hebrew: "sound"), properly understanding and holding to Your Decrees (Statutes) so that no one will be able to accuse Me of falling short in My mission to save the Church."

- This is a statement that closes (concludes) and encompasses all the thoughts and pleas of this octet. It reflects the full weight of the burden that rests on Jesus, our King and Savior, to be faithful to His mission which was in part to repudiate Satan's proposition to Eve. He is undoing the Fall. Behold, He makes all things new!

Question for you: If Jesus had ever chosen to figure out and implement, on His own, a solution to a problem He had instead of waiting for YHWH to reveal it to Him from His word, would He still have been qualified to save us?

כ **Kaph (20)** – Theme: In My severe affliction and agony I seek comfort, hope, and relief from Your word.

81. "My soul faints with longing for your salvation,
   but I have put my hope in your word." (NIV)

   Hebrew Literal: "<u>Faints</u>   <u>for your salvation</u>   <u>my soul</u> – <u>for your word</u>
                      <u>I hope</u>."

Meditations and commentary:

- Behold: The incarnate God—the Christ!!!

- This verse and Vv. 82 & 87 paint a picture of a man who has trusted YHWH beyond his point of last endurance. Yes! He has identified with my weakness (which is His strength!)!

- Oh, I mourn, but I should rejoice, that the Lord of Glory, my Lord, should endure such suffering, but He has endured it for me and my brothers and sisters.

- When reading this octet, I am reminded of the lines that Dickens wrote to open his book *Tale of Two Cities*: "It was the best of times, it was the worst of times..." Only for this octet, I would reverse those two thoughts and say, "It was the worst of times, it was the best of times."

   I can barely read this octet because of the depth of the pain and suffering being experienced by Jesus. In this octet, He is experiencing very great tribulation that
   - Pushes Him past His point of last strength (v. 81)
   - Pushes Him past His point of last understanding (v. 82)
   - Pushes Him past His point of good health (v. 83)
   - Pushes Him nearly past His point of last endurance (v. 87)

- In this octet, Jesus is at His lowest level of existence; but at this point of great suffering, He demonstrates unwavering commitment to, and hope in, the words that proceed from the mouth of YHWH. In this way, He is securing righteousness for us, because in this way He is proving the validity of trusting in the words and provisions of God through His Commands, Statutes, and Precepts. His commitment accomplishes the repudiation of Satan's proposition to Eve (see Chapter 2 of this book). It accomplishes our deliverance from that lie. It establishes Christ as the worthy deliverer and savior of His Church—those who trust in the testimony of His demonstrated commitment to be the provisions of God (through His word). The eternal paradox: when Jesus was at His lowest point of suffering, He was at His highest exaltation.

Question for you: Have you ever considered that maybe you are most useful in God's hands when you are in the midst of great failure in your life?

82. "My eyes fail, looking for your promise;
    I say, 'When will you comfort me?'" (NIV)

Hebrew Literal: "<u>Strain</u>   <u>my eyes</u>   <u>for your spoken word</u> – <u>saying</u>
                    <u>when will you</u>   <u>comfort me</u>?"

Meditations and commentary:

- Christ, the King, is demonstrating the <u>validity</u> of trusting in YHWH and His Word (v. 81), even though deliverance is beyond what He can see. This is a repudiation of the Eve temptation (as outlined in Chapter 2).

- We are drawn to rally to our King as He suffers so deeply! When we suffer like this from now on, we will know that our suffering is divine, because Jesus' suffering was divine! (See John 10:31-38 below.) There is nothing wrong with us when we fail to see God's deliverance; in those moments, we are being like Christ! Despite what we see, we <u>trust</u> that God is faithful! We trust that He will deliver us! This is the mind and heart of Christ. (Even if deliverance comes through death as it was with Christ at the end of His earthly life.)

- In John 10:31-38 says,

  > **31** Again his Jewish opponents picked up stones to stone him,
  > **32** but Jesus said to them, "I have shown you many good works from the Father. For which of these do you stone me?"
  > **33** "We are not stoning you for any good work," they replied, "but for blasphemy, because you, a mere man, claim to be God."
  > **34** Jesus answered them, "Is it not written in your Law, **'I have said you are "gods" '**?
  > **35** If **he called them 'gods,'** to whom the word of God came—and **Scripture cannot be set aside**—

36 what about the one whom the Father set apart as his very own and sent into the world? Why then do you accuse me of blasphemy because I said, 'I am God's Son'?

37 Do not believe me unless I do the works of my Father.

38 But if I do them, even though you do not believe me, believe the works, that you may know and understand that the Father is in me, and I in the Father."

Question for you: In His prayer to YHWH in verse 81, Jesus refers to Scripture as "your word," but in His prayer in this verse (v. 82), Jesus refers to Scripture as "your spoken word." Why do you think Jesus sometimes calls Scripture the "word" of YHWH, and other times He calls it the "spoken word" of YHWH?

83. "Though I am like a wineskin in the smoke
    I do not forget your decrees." (NIV)

Hebrew Literal: "For   I have become   like a wineskin   in the smoke –
              Your statutes   not   do I forget."

Meditations and commentary:

- This verse is a continuation of the previous verse.

- His soul was enduring slow destruction as He weathered these trials. His soul was being dried out, turning brittle, weakened, and He was watching it fail. Even so, He was NOT persuaded to rescue Himself, but to trust in YHWH's deliverance as provided for by YHWH's decrees. One example of this is found in Matthew 4:1-4 where He says, "Man does not live by bread alone, but by every word that proceeds from the mouth of God."

- Jesus is my King! This is the repudiation of Satan's proposition to Eve! (see Chapter 2) He is replacing the Fall with a new life that trusts in the spoken word of YHWH for all of its provisions.

Question for you: Like Jesus, do you sometimes have to face the fact that your life is in the process of being destroyed? Like Jesus, when you face this realization, do you find comfort in the Statutes and Decrees of God as they appear in Scripture?

84. "How long must your servant wait?
    When will you punish my persecutors?" (NIV)

    Hebrew Literal: "How many [are]   the days   of your servant ?
    When   will you execute   on those who persecute me
    judgment?"

Meditations and commentary:

- I do not like to think too much about this verse because:
  - I am one of the persecutors of Jesus.
  - My punishment is on Him. Jesus is praying here, longing for, His crucifixion and the wrath of God to be poured out on Him for my sake. "Greater love has no man that this: that he lay down his life for his friends" (John 15:13).

- Jesus is my savior! He is demonstrating that the love of God is greater and stronger than the evil of Satan. He is a fully incarnate man who overcomes the evil of Satan. What a splendid and marvelous King!

Question for you: In what ways do you persecute Jesus?

85. "The arrogant dig pitfalls for me,
    contrary to your law." (NIV)

    Hebrew Literal: "Have dug   for me   the proud   pits –
    that   not [are]   according to your law."

Meditations and commentary:

- Examples of the pitfalls (these should sound familiar to us):
  - "What! Are you crazy?! You have the power to deliver yourself, so do it! What kind of presumption is this: 'I am waiting on YHWH to deliver me?!' Don't be a fool! Climb out of that hole because you can!"
  - "God gave you a mind and a will of your own! Use it! (Exert yourself and decide what to do—that which seems best to you, instead of waiting for God to deliver you!)
  - Frank Sinatra's song, "I did it my way."
  - "You are an independent adult! Act like it!"

- o "What does it matter if you bend that commandment (of God) just a little bit to give you some practical relief? Surely it's not that big a thing to cheat just a little. You deserve this."
- o And here's the one that gets me: "If you didn't violate this little command of God to relieve some of the pressure, then you will end up violating this bigger command of God; and then you'll have a <u>real</u> mess."
- o "Do you always have to be so anal about doing everything precisely right?"
- o "Are you so arrogant that you believe your personal convictions are more important than the counsel and needs of the whole group?"
- o "The power, will, and legitimacy of the civil government are more important than your personal private convictions."
- Jesus stands as an unassailable contradiction to all of the above expressions of arrogance.

Question for you: Which of the above listed arrogances seem most compelling for you?

86. "All your commands are trustworthy;
     Help me, for men persecute me without cause." (NIV)

     Hebrew Literal: "<u>All</u> <u>your commands [are]</u> <u>faith</u>.
                      <u>With falsehood</u> <u>they persecute me</u> -- <u>help me</u>."

Meditations and commentary:

- The second line of the Hebrew Literal begs the question: "What is the falsehood they are using to persecute Jesus?" The answer is in the previous verse (v. 85).

- (following from v. 85) But... <u>All</u> your commands are trustworthy. None of them are to be minimized. None of them are to be discarded in favor of the others! So, <u>help me YHWH</u>, because the power of the mighty and influential is trying to get me to compromise.

- Jesus does not attempt to remain faithful in only His own strength, but even in this He seeks the help and provision of YHWH.

Question for you: When you are tempted, do you try to resist the temptation by trying really hard to avoid it, or do you search Scripture asking God to show you how He has already provided the way of escape? Which approach did Jesus use?

87. "They almost wiped me from the earth,
    But I have not forsaken your precepts." (NIV)

    Hebrew Literal: "Almost   they had consumed me   on earth—
                    but I   not   do did forsake   your precepts."

Meditations and commentary:

- I was out of strength and they almost caused me to fail in my mission, but in the end, I did NOT compromise! I did not give up relying on the wisdom of Your Precepts.

- Had Jesus only compromised a little, then all of humanity would be lost and Satan's proposition (see Chapter 2) would have been validated, and the strength of YHWH among men would have failed. Praise be to Jesus who saved us by His unwavering trust in YHWH and His word!

- His unwavering, uncompromising trust in the Precepts of YHWH is something I cannot do, so Jesus did it for me!

Question for you: Do you think this was a frequent struggle for Jesus, that He was "almost wiped" from the earth? Would it surprise you to discover that He faced this more often than you do?

88. "Preserve my life according to your love,
    And I will obey the statutes of your mouth." (NIV)

    Hebrew Literal: "In your covenant loyalty   revive me —
                    so shall I keep   the testimony   of your mouth."

Meditations and commentary:

- This train of thought (from vv. 81-87) must necessarily end in the double realization of the facts that:
    - YHWH will preserve the life of the obedient Christ because of the love of YHWH (not because of the obedience of Christ)—this is grace in operation in the God-head; and
    - Jesus must continue to be the absolutely consistently obedient Messiah, the one who trusts in every word that proceeds from the mouth of YHWH. This defines their two roles, and it defines these roles in the face of unrelenting and excruciating tribulation.

- In the next octet, in v. 92, Jesus says, "If <u>Your Law</u> had not been my delight, I would have perished in my affliction." Was Christ's obedience to the statutes of God a clenched-teeth, stone-faced, duty-bound hard disciplined adherence, or was it an enthusiastic, passionate, delightful grasping for every nuance of the statutes of YHWH, delivered in His great (infinite) love? We who are in Christ have also experienced this same reassuring comfort. When in the midst of unbearable suffering, the only real comfort and consolation we find is when we go to the word of God in the Scriptures and let the Holy Spirit minister to us from His word. Even we have known the strength and comfort and refuge of our loving God that comes to us in this way from His Word. In this way, even we experience what Christ experienced in the midst of His suffering.

Question for you: Do you ever feel like God should bless your life because you have been obedient to Him? Do you understand that feelings (and expectations) like that are part of your fallen nature, and not ever the way Jesus thought?

Copyright © 2018, Richard L. Routh, All rights reserved.

ל **Lamedh (30)** – Theme: Unless Your faithful Law had been My delight, I would have perished in My affliction.

89. "Your word, YHWH, is eternal,
It stands firm in the heavens." (NIV)

Hebrew Literal: "<u>Forever</u>   <u>YHWH</u>   <u>your word</u>   <u>stands</u>
<u>in heaven</u>."

Meditations and commentary:

- Most translations use the word "forever," but some very modern translations have begun using the word "eternal" here. In my opinion, this is a valid trend.

- The word of YHWH is not only useful (applicable) on earth, but it is also useful in heaven. More than useful, it is consistently and unshakably prescriptive.

- The word of YHWH is not only useful in this age, but it is also useful in the age(s) to come (Eph 1:21). It will be useful to us in the new heaven and the new earth (Rev 21:1).

Question for you: Can you think of some specific ways in which the Old Testament Scriptures will be useful to us in the New Earth, when there is no longer any sin?

90. "Your faithfulness continues through all generations;
You established the earth, and it endures." (NIV)

Hebrew Literal: "<u>To generation</u>   <u>and generation</u>   <u>[is] your faithfulness –</u>
<u>you have established</u>   <u>the earth</u>   <u>and it stays</u>."

Meditations and commentary:

- This is a proclamation, even celebration, of the faithfulness of God.

- Is the establishment and endurance of the earth given as evidence of the faithfulness of God? If so, then why is this in a psalm where nearly every verse contains some reference to the word of God? Because the earth and all it contains came into existence, was created, by the spoken word of God (Genesis 1). This is thereby a testimony of the weight, importance, and permanence of the word of God.

- Note: There will always be an earth; either this one or the new one.

Question for you: Do you think God requires you to remember the things you asked Him for long ago in order for Him to continue working out their fulfillment? In other words, are there some prayers you made long ago that God is still answering even though you have forgotten that you ever asked Him for those petitions?

91. "Your laws endure to this day,
For all things serve you." (NIV)

Hebrew Literal: "According to your judgments   they continue   this day –
for   all things   [are] your servants."

Meditations and commentary:

- This verse can be translated as: "All things serve you according to your laws, which endure even to this day, [so that they are eminently applicable even in this modern time]."

- In other words, in order for anything to operate/function properly, it must function as the Laws of YHWH prescribe.

- Since God is omniscient and eternal and sovereign, He is able to announce laws that will always work in all situations across all of time—and that is what He has done. Such are the laws of God!

Question for you: This octet is, in part, a response to the previous octet. How is the enduring applicability of the Laws of YHWH an encouraging answer to the severe agony expressed in the previous octet (vv. 81-88)?

92. "If your law had not been my delight,
I would have perished in my affliction." (NIV)

Hebrew Literal: "Unless   your law   [had been] my delights,
                then   I should have perished   in my affliction."

Meditations and commentary:

- (Please see the commentary written about v. 88 in the previous octet.)

- Jesus is acknowledging that His survival through His affliction depends on Him not only aligning all His actions with the Law of YHWH, but also on His heart attitude. His heart delights in God's Law and His survival (in His incarnation) depends on that delighting.

- I praise you Lord Jesus that you always delight in the Law of YHWH and that you do so for me and my brothers and sisters. You have accomplished that delighting for us, in our stead, so that we will forever be treated by God as though we had always delighted in His Law!

Question for you: Do you think God is interested in our obedience to His Law from a sense of duty? Or is He only interested when we obey from a sense of delight in His Law?

93. "I will never forget your precepts,
     For by them you have preserved [revived] my life." (NIV)

Hebrew Literal: "Ever   not   will I forget   your precepts,
                for   by them   you have revived me."

Meditations and commentary:

- The Hebrew word here translated "preserved" is the word "revived." Not only is Jesus acknowledging the Precepts of YHWH as the means of His rescue from the troubles recounted in the previous octet, but Jesus is proclaiming that His resurrection is provided for by the Precepts of YHWH. He, and therefore we, are eternally dependent on the relevance of the Precepts of God.

- Praise be to Jesus who has consistently conformed to, and relied on, the Precepts of God. He did that for us, and that is our hope!

Question for you: If the Laws of YHWH are forever applicable and important, then what is the meaning of Colossians 2:14 when it says, God "cancelled the written code, with its regulations, that was against us and that stood opposed to us; he took it away, nailing it to the cross"?

94. "Save me, for I am yours;
  I have sought out your precepts." (NIV)

  Hebrew Literal: "To you I am save me for your precepts
                    I have sought."

Meditations and commentary:

- Jesus said in Luke 6:46, "Why do you call me, 'Lord, Lord,' and do not do what I say?" It is the same thought expressed here. It is the Father's role to save all that which belongs to Him, and it is the Son's role to seek out the precepts of His Father. The Father delights to save Jesus (and thereby all of us who are in Christ) and it is the delight of Jesus (v. 92) to seek out and follow all the precepts of His Father.

  Question for you: If Jesus "sought out" the Precepts of YHWH, then does that searching imply that there were things to understand about YHWH's Precepts that Jesus did not yet understand?

95. "The wicked are waiting to destroy me,
  But I will ponder your statutes." (NIV)

  Hebrew Literal: "For me have waited the wicked to destroy –
                    your testimonies I will consider."

Meditations and commentary:

- In the Hebrew, this verse literally says the wicked have waited "for me" to destroy me. In other words, the wicked are lurking and searching for their opportunity to destroy Jesus. An opportunity that Jesus knows will come when they finally crucify Him. But Jesus' focus, from which He no doubt gets hope and encouragement, is on the testimonies (statutes) of YHWH which testify to His resurrection and victory over the effects **_on us_** of sin and evil.

Question for you: Can you list some of the ways in which Jesus has freed you from the <u>effects</u> of sin and evil? *NOTE: In your answer, it would be helpful to list things other than your behaviors (other than your actions and activities).*

96. "To all perfection I see a limit;
    But your commands are boundless." (NIV)

Hebrew Literal: "<u>To all   perfection   I have seen   a limit</u> –
              <u>[but] broad   [is] your command   exceedingly</u>."

Meditations and commentary:

- Only the commands of YHWH are infinitely applicable. Every other thing that is properly and wholly complete (perfect) is either perfect only in itself, or perfect for some particular situation (or limited set of situations), or perfect for some set (and limited) time-frame.

  But the commands of YHWH are NOT limited by time, or situation, or scope. The commands of YHWH are properly applicable to all things, in all situations, across all times, in heaven or on earth.

- This understanding of the boundless applicability of the Laws of YHWH must have been a great encouragement and motivation for Jesus to pour His full heart and commitment into seeking and following the commands of YHWH. Praise be to Jesus for consistently having that attitude, because He has accomplished this consistency for us (in our place). God now attributes to us all the merits and consequences of having consistently maintained this perspective and attitude in our hearts and in our wills. Jesus has accomplished this for us!

Questions for you:
When your life begins to fall apart and you desperately need something steady and stable to hold onto, do you ever consider that you might find that needed stability in the Commands of God? What would that look like for you?

Often we think of the Commands of God as being the Ten Commandments, but there are many other Commands of God in Scripture. For example, can you list the Commands of God that appear in the first two chapters of the Book of Genesis? (We count at least 22 specific "spoken by God" Commands.)

מ **Mem (40)** – Theme: I am focused ONLY on trusting You through Your word. Nothing else that I could be doing matters.

97. "Oh, how I love your law!
    I meditate on it all day long." (NIV)

> Hebrew Literal: "<u>Oh how</u>   <u>I love</u>   <u>your law</u>
>   <u>All</u>   <u>the day</u>   <u>it</u>   <u>[is] my meditation</u>."

Meditations and commentary:

- Most people's experience, when they first meet their life's mate, is to think about that person constantly. You are excited about being with them and that thought occupies your mind all day long.

- Jesus does not see the Law of YHWH as some lifeless code of behavior. He sees the Law as the key to understanding the identity of the Father. The person of the Father has been revealed in the Law that has been spoken from His mouth. If you want to experientially know God, then study His character and His values and His heart as they are revealed in His Law (consider this in the light of John 17:3).

- Jesus sees the Law as the means to the revelation of the person of the Father. "Know the Law" means: see the Father for Who He truly is.

- Jesus is so in love with YHWH that He is drawn to constantly search the Law of YHWH for new insights into the character and person of YHWH. That is why He meditates on the Law all day long. It is not a "duty" for Him; it is because He is in LOVE!

  Question for you: Do you find it surprising that the reason Jesus constantly meditates on the Law of YHWH is because He is in love?

98. "Your commands make me wiser than my enemies,
    for they are ever with me." (NIV)

Hebrew Literal: "Than my enemies   you have made me wiser
            through your commands   for [are]   ever   they   with me."

Meditations and commentary:

- Jesus knows that YHWH's Law and His Commands prescribe how everything in life operates. We study the laws of physics because they give us the understanding we need to produce the various technologies we have. Our cars, our heating and air conditioning, our electricity, lights, our mobile devices, the Internet, our airplanes and satellites, our medical technologies, all are possible because we understand and apply the laws of physics.

- Jesus knows the Laws and Commands of YHWH give a person that same type of understanding and advantage as they encounter the various challenges of life. The person who knows and applies the Commands of YHWH in their life has a very great advantage over those who do not. The enemies of God are at a distinct disadvantage compared to those who learn the Commands of God.

Question for you: Have you ever considered that an effective way to become more successful in life is to learn and apply more of the Commands of God?

99. "I have more insight than [all] my teachers,
    for I meditate on your statutes." (NIV)

Hebrew Literal: "Than all   my teachers   I have more understanding
            for   your testimonies [are]   meditation   to me."

Meditations and commentary:

- If you were to ask Jesus, "Where does insight come from?" He would answer, "Insight comes from meditating on the Statutes of YHWH."

- And then if you were to ask Him, "Where does understanding come from?" He would answer, "Understanding comes from keeping the Precepts of YHWH" (v. 100).

- Those who were Jesus' teachers evidently sought insight from sources other than the Statutes of YHWH. This was not a mistake Jesus made.

- One of the consequences of Adam and Eve accepting Satan's proposition, and the subsequent Fall of mankind, was the choosing to be relegated to getting our insights from our own inferences of our own experiences and observations. Jesus is saying here that He has demonstrated the superiority of the strategy of getting insight from the Statutes of God, instead of from the inferences of our own experiences and observations.

Question for you: Do you trust more in the Statutes and Testimonies of God than you do in your own experiences? How would Jesus answer this question?

100. "I have more understanding than the elders,
for I obey your precepts." (NIV)

Hebrew Literal: "<u>More than the ancients</u>　<u>I understand</u>
<u>because</u>　<u>your precepts</u>　<u>I keep</u>."

Meditations and commentary:

- (Continuing from the commentary of the previous verse) And likewise, one of the consequences of accepting Satan's proposition was the choosing to be relegated to getting our understanding from our own experiences (i.e.—trusting and valuing our own experiences more than we trust and value God's Precepts). This self-referent perspective is the inherited predisposition that convinces us of the merit of embracing Satan's proposition in our lives. Doesn't it just feel right to think we should be doing our best to be good? Doesn't it just seem to be common sense to think we should trust in our own experiences and our own best thinking? Those feelings are all you need to prove to yourself that your fallen nature is strong.

- But Jesus is saying here that He has demonstrated a better way to get understanding (better than inferring it from our own experiences). That better way is to get understanding from embracing the Precepts of YHWH.

- One of the demonstrations of the loving, compassionate provision of God for us is through the meditation on His Statutes and the keeping of His Precepts because this gets us further than we could get if all we had was being relegated to figuring things out on our own based on whatever we thought was the right way to extract insight and understanding from our own experiences and other observations.

Behold the Christ　　Copyright © 2018, Richard L. Routh, All rights reserved.

- Somewhere along the way here we need to grapple with the realization that what's important in our lives is not how smart we are, but how well we know God; and what's important is not how we are obeying God, but how we are trusting Him.

Question for you: What would a college curriculum look like that was focused exclusively on discovering the insights buried in Scripture and then teaching how to apply those in all the different challenges of everyday life?

101. "I have kept my feet from every evil path
so that I might obey your word." (NIV)

Hebrew Literal: "From every   way   evil   I have restrained   my feet
to the end that   I might keep   your word."

Meditations and commentary:

- This verse needs to be seen in conjunction with v. 105—the first verse of the next octet, and it needs to be seen as a consequence of the previous two verses (vv. 99 & 100).

- An evil path is anything that would influence us (Jesus, in this case) to NOT rely on the word of YHWH. In the light of the previous two verses, Jesus is saying that it is important for Him to NOT seek insight and understanding from any other source (including our best thinking about our own observations and experiences). This is an extraordinary conclusion and completely goes against our nature! (See also John 8:28.)

Question for you: How does John 8:28 confirm the above statement?

102. "I have not departed from your laws,
for you yourself have taught me." (NIV)

Hebrew Literal: "From your judgments   not   do I have departed
for   you   have taught me."

Meditations and commentary:

- When the sovereign creator of the heavens and the earth (and the timeline) decides to do something, it gets done. Furthermore, it gets done not as though it were an impersonal task, but YHWH's personality and compassion and care are intimately involved and fully engaged in everything He does.

- Here Jesus is recognizing and celebrating the fact that YHWH has made an eternal personal commitment to (He has bound Himself to) providing the <u>completely effectual</u> teaching of His Laws to Jesus Christ.

- Jesus does recognize that He Himself has a role to play in that He (Jesus) must not depart from YHWH's Laws. But Jesus is also recognizing here that He does not accomplish this by Himself. The Father has a role to play here, and the Father's role is to teach the Son so effectively that the Son's adherence to the laws of YHWH is (eternally) assured. IT IS, and always has been, AN ETERNAL PARTNERSHIP.

Question for you: In light of the roles outlined above, how is it that The Father would call The Son His (The Father's) God (as He does in Hebrews 1:8)?

103. "How sweet are your words to my taste,
     sweeter than honey to my mouth." (NIV)

Hebrew Literal: "<u>How   sweet   to my taste   are your words</u>
          <u>[sweeter] than honey   to my mouth</u>."

Meditations and commentary:

- (continuing from v. 102) And Jesus' adherence to the Laws of God is not an impersonal discipline and duty. Jesus' keeping of the Laws of YHWH is a celebration of a deeply personal love relationship—the words of YHWH are love letters written from the Father to the Son, and Jesus received them as such.

- So, I restate this because it is a central theme and key to understanding Jesus' attitude towards the Laws of YHWH (as given through Moses and the prophets): For Jesus, the Laws of God were NOT impersonal tasks to be accomplished; they were not burdensome duties to be performed; but they are the compassionate provisions of YHWH to be lovingly embraced. The Laws of YHWH are not separable from the personality of YHWH and both are absolutely full of love and compassion (as well as holiness).

Question for you: Do the Ten Commandments seem like a love letter to you?

104. "I gain understanding from your precepts;
   therefore I hate every wrong path." (NIV)

Hebrew Literal: "<u>From your precepts</u>   <u>I get understanding</u>
                  <u>therefore</u>   <u>thus</u>   <u>I hate</u>   <u>every</u>   <u>way</u>   <u>false</u>."

Meditations and commentary:

- "Wrong" is defined here as anything that does not come from the Precepts of YHWH.

- "Wrong" is what Adam and Eve chose when they chose to allow "good" to be defined by themselves, instead of trusting YHWH to tell them what "good" was.

- Jesus hates the proposition that we should be allowed to have an opinion (that differs from God's decrees) as to what is fair. Our opinions, and our corresponding fallen nature, are in opposition to the wisdom and goodness of God, and Jesus wants no part of the proposition that we (or He as an incarnate man) should be allowed to have a self-defined opinion on what is fair.

- The precepts of God give understanding—not our experiences, observations and opinions. So, here in verse 104 is another example of Jesus repudiating the proposition Satan presented to Eve.

Question for you: Is it possible to find true and useful understanding from any source that does not align with the word of God? What aligns with the word of God better than Scripture?

ב Nun (50) – Theme: My heart rejoices because Your Law is my eternal inheritance!

105. "Your word is a lamp to my feet
and a light for my path." (NIV)

Hebrew Literal: "<u>A lamp</u>   <u>to my feet</u>   <u>your word [is]</u>
                        <u>and a light</u>   <u>to my path</u>."

Meditations and commentary:

- I can't read this verse without hearing in my head it being sung by Amy Grant.

- For Jesus, the word of YHWH was His map that He could rely on to know which next step to take and in what direction He should take it.

- I am not familiar enough, intimately acquainted enough, with the word of YHWH such that it informs me of what and how I should think and say and do in every situation. But evidently, Jesus was that familiar with the word of YHWH. I praise Him that He was that intimately acquainted with the word of YHWH, and that He relied on YHWH's word to inform His every step. He accomplished that for me and my brothers and sisters so that we can now rest without anxiety in His finished work! Praise be to our God (Father, Son, and Holy Spirit) who has provided complete righteousness for us!

  Question for you: When you find yourself thinking (and feeling) that you are more righteous when you are obedient to the word of God, do you realize that faulty thinking is a natural error that comes from your fallen nature? Have you noticed that when you are walking by the Spirit (your new nature) that you are not inclined to think (or feel) such things?

106. "I have taken an oath and confirmed it,
that I will follow your righteous laws." (NIV)

Hebrew Literal: "<u>I have sworn</u>   <u>that I will confirm</u>
                        <u>I will keep</u>   <u>your judgments</u>   <u>righteous</u>."

Meditations and commentary:

- This oath that Jesus took originated in the counsels of the God-head from the infinite halls of eternity.

- Consider a conversation something like this taking place:
  Father (speaking to the Son): "It is Our intent to provide everything that mankind will need, including their righteousness. Satan will convince them to attempt to achieve righteousness on their own. They will accept his offer, but will be unable to accomplish it. This attempt will so blind them that they will not even know how far off they are. So, I will give them My Law which will convict them of how far short they have fallen.

  "Satan will have thought he has made the cosmic case that it is unreasonable to want mankind to be righteous. Based on their failure, he will think he has proven that they should be completely destroyed and the plan to create them for intimate fellowship with Us is not a reasonable one.

  "Your job, Jesus, will be to go down there as a man, as one of them, as My second Adam, to live a life completely righteously in accordance with the Laws I will have given them. In this way, You will refute Satan's argument that it is not reasonable that a man could live a fully righteous life—one that is completely dependent on Us.

  "Once You have proven for all to see that it is possible and desirable for a man to be fully righteous by trusting Me and My word more than one trusts his own human faculties and judgments, then I will pour out My wrath onto You, in their place, for their sin, and in this way, You will accomplish Our provision of righteousness for them.

  "Those who accept your provision of righteousness for themselves will then have the righteousness You have accomplished for them and provided to them."

  Son: "Yes, I promise I will do all this so they can be one with Us even as I am in You and You are in Me. I swear now with My oath that I will do this, and I will confirm this oath when I am down there accomplishing righteousness for them."

  Me: "I do praise You and thank You, Lord Jesus, because You have accomplished and provided righteousness for me and my brothers and sisters! YOU have completed all the work and there is nothing left for us to accomplish. We are now free to walk in the righteousness You have provided to us! Praise be to our God!"

Question for you: When Christians think they achieve greater righteousness through their obedience to the Laws of God, what does that imply about their opinion of the sufficiency of what was provided to them by Christ?

107. "I have suffered much;
preserve my life, YHWH, according to your word." (NIV)

Hebrew Literal: "<u>I am afflicted</u>   <u>very</u>   <u>much</u>
<u>YHWH</u>   <u>revive me</u>   <u>according to your word</u>."

Meditations and commentary:

- Where does Jesus' suffering come from? Let us list a few of the sources:

  - The incessant testimony of men that strict adherence to, and the complete passionate embracing of, the Law of God is an unreasonable (even insane) commitment. Jesus genuinely loves the people around Him and deeply desires a bonding fellowship with them, but that fellowship is constantly being violated by betrayal. To be constantly stabbed in the back by those with whom you want fellowship, is an incessant grievous suffering. A wife who finds herself enduring the continual philandering of a womanizing husband, one who has promised to remain faithful to her, is familiar with this type of suffering. She commits her heart to him, but he repeatedly stomps on it, thereby crushing her soul and causing her to find ugliness and poison and darkness for her soul where there was supposed to be hope, and love, and strength, and light. It was this type of suffering, and it was unrelenting, that Jesus Christ continually endured. He wanted genuine fellowship and friendship with those who would treasure the love and provision of the Father, as He did. But instead, He got those who desired to be independent from YHWH; those who despised what He loved; those whose last (read: "never") thought (desire) was to embrace the commands of YHWH as the guiding provision for their lives.

  - Another type of suffering that Jesus endured was having His heart continually broken as He witnessed a world that was so deeply and grievously marred by the damage that sin had brought. Sickness and death are consequences of sin. They were not part of the world when it was originally created by God, but when sin entered the human experience, along with it came sickness and death, hunger and starvation, divorce, abused children, sex trafficking, adultery, birth defects, depression, malice, murder and hatred. Along with these painful tragedies that directly affect people who were originally created in the image of the Holy, pure, loving, good God, was also the marring of all that mankind had authority over: animals were treated cruelly and abused and killed, in so many ugly ways; forests were wantonly decimated; the earth was ruined and degraded from its initial beauty in so many heartbreaking ways. Whole species of magnificent animals were brought to extinction. The list goes on and on. As Jesus witnessed all of this that is not as it was initially intended to be by its Creator; it was no longer an accurate reflection and testimony of the goodness and glory of God, and He suffered much because of it.

- In order to keep from being completely discouraged and wiped from the face of the earth, Jesus kept His focus on the only completely pure and unmarred thing there was: the word of YHWH—YHWH's Law, Testimonies, Precepts, Commandments. Only these were perfect and pure and Holy and unaffected by sin. Only by staring constantly at them, was Jesus' Spirit preserved in the face of the great damage and destruction brought on by sin.

- The person and the character of the Holy, Holy, Holy, Lord God, Almighty, Who was, and is, and is to come, is not marred by sin, and He who would stare intently into His Law and His Testimonies will see the unmarred beauty of God. That is the secret to being lifted out of despair.

- Jesus said, "Blessed are those who mourn, because they shall be comforted." Yes, blessed are those who mourn the effects of sin, for they shall be comforted by the saving work of Christ as He stares intently into the word of YHWH and conforms in every way to the Law of YHWH and thereby rises above sin and death and all its ugliness, and thereby nullifies the judgments of sin on this world. Praise be to the Lord Jesus Christ who has rescued us from the ugly effects of sin!

Question for you: What causes you to mourn?

108. "Accept, YHWH, the willing praise of my mouth,
and teach me your laws." (NIV)

Hebrew Literal: "The freewill offerings   of my mouth   accept
I beseech you   YHWH   and your judgments   teach me."

Meditations and commentary:

- One of the great gifts YHWH gives us is the privilege to praise Him. I am convinced that the difference between YHWH and people is so extreme that, except for God's sacrificial graciousness to us, it would make no sense at all for us to think there could be any communication between people and YHWH. YHWH chooses to humble Himself to even notice us, let alone to allow us to commune with Him.

- God is, and must be, the initiator of communication with people. He is so extremely Holy that He would be otherwise unapproachable by us.

- It is only because Jesus, the second person of the Godhead (in other words: God Himself), prays to YHWH for Him to accept our praise, that we are even able to praise Him in such a way that He will listen and accept it. Jesus, in so praying here in v. 108, opens the door for people to praise YHWH.

- Even when a high earthly authority, which is much less high than the creator of heaven and earth and the sovereign ruler of the entire timeline (Who was and is and is to come the Lord God, Almighty), chooses to publicly communicate with an individual, it focuses his entire organization, at least for that moment, on that individual. For example, when the President of the United States picks up his telephone and calls the widow of a fallen soldier, it is not just an individual person calling another individual person, but because of his job, he chooses by his act to focus the attention of the entire nation on that fallen soldier and his widow. It is reported by the press; it is commented on by the news commentators, and millions of people have their eyes and thoughts, at least momentarily, focused on that widow. By necessity, it elevates the social value of that widow to those who have the attention and respect of the entire nation.

- In this same way, when YHWH chooses to not only pay attention to, but even to accept, the praise of our lips and hearts, which are directed to Him, then by this very act He focuses the attention of all of heaven and earth, past, present and future, on us at that moment of praise. It is not our praising God that gives us this eternal attention and value, but it is God's choosing to accept our praise that gives us this eternal attention and value. And YHWH would have no legitimate justification to accept our praise except for the fact that Jesus opens the door for us by His petition in our place. Those of us who are in Christ, now have this standing before YHWH, and we therefore now have the assurance, because of the finished work of Christ, that YHWH does accept our praise when it is willingly offered. Praise be to the Lord Jesus Christ who has given us this extreme exalted position to be able to receive the attention and acceptance of YHWH and all who pay attention to Him (at least all the angelic host of heaven)!

- But it does not stop here. The gracious provision of the God of all eternity does not stop with extending to us the extreme value that is bestowed on us by His attention and focus on us. It also includes, because of Jesus' petition here in v. 108, YHWH communing with us and His personal attention and care and provision to instruct us in His Law. And we saw in the commentary on the previous verse (v. 107) that His Law is a gift of the highest and most pure value. When YHWH is teaching us His Law, He is in fact, carrying out the fulfillment of the request made by Christ in John 17:20-23: "Just as You are in Me and I am in You, may they also be in Us!"

- And what does Jesus mean, "Teach Me Your Laws"? What's to teach? Isn't it pretty simple and straightforward and obvious that when YHWH says, "Thou shalt not commit adultery" that He means just and precisely what He says? So, what's to teach? Jesus says that the Law of God goes deeper than just what it appears to be on the surface. For example, in Matthew 5:27-28, the command to not commit adultery also means that we shall not lust. And He says in Matthew 5:21-22, the command to not murder also means that we are not to hate another person, and not to even speak disparagingly about them. How are we going to properly understand all the deeper meanings of the Law of God unless the Spirit of God teaches us? Furthermore, one has not "learned" a new concept until it is properly applied in one's life. The request for YHWH to teach us His Law includes a request for Him to guide us through the process of properly applying it in our lives.

- Furthermore, the testimony of v. 108 is that Jesus has properly praised YHWH, YHWH has accepted His praise, and YHWH has taught Jesus His Law, to include its proper application in the life of the incarnate Christ. In this way, Jesus Christ has fulfilled these requirements of the Law for us. The pressure for us to perform has been completely removed by Christ. He has opened the doors of heaven for us and we are now free to praise God, knowing that He will accept our willing praise and will teach us His Law, which most certainly **is predicated on our reliance on the finished work of Jesus Christ**.

Question for you: Do you understand that when you obey the Laws of God, your obedience is a gift from God to you, and it is **NOT** a gift from you to God?

109. "Though I constantly take my life in my hands,
    I will not forget your law." (NIV)

Hebrew Literal: "<u>My life</u>   [is] <u>in my hands</u>   <u>continually</u>
<u>and your law</u>   <u>not</u>   <u>do will I forget</u>."

Meditations and commentary:

- To "take one's life in one's hands" means to "risk one's life."

- Jesus is acknowledging here that His life is continually being put at risk. Remember He says in v. 95 that the wicked are lurking and looking for an opportunity to destroy Him, and they are doing so because of His constant unwavering commitment to the Statutes of YHWH.

- The word "though" as it appears at the beginning of this verse in the NIV is not in the literal Hebrew, but the translator has assumed that it is implied by the Hebrew and inserted it to help us see the implication of logical dependency here. But if the relationship between these two clauses is assumed to be different (since the Hebrew is not specific), then this verse could be translated: The result of Me not forgetting Your law is that it constantly puts My life at risk. This is in contrast to the interpretation that: Your Law offers Me remedy and refuge in the face of the constant risk I face and I will not neglect to accept that remedy and refuge. Or: There is a third possibility and that is that these two clauses are linked in such a way that they are both logically dependent on the other. In that case, the picture here would be one of a spiraling ascending dependency—that is: The more I follow Your Law, the more My life is put at risk, and the more My life is put at risk, the more important it is for Me to seek the proper course of action from Your Law for My protection. I suspect, because of the context of the rest of Psalm 119, that the third interpretation is intended.

Question for you: How do you think it felt for Jesus to have His life constantly being put at risk? (Note: This is not a rhetorical question.)

110. "The wicked have set a snare for me,
but I have not strayed from your precepts." (NIV)

Hebrew Literal: "<u>Have laid</u>   <u>the wicked</u>   <u>a snare</u>   <u>for me</u>
<u>and from your precepts</u>   <u>not</u>   <u>do have I strayed</u>."

Meditations and commentary:

- Whenever we leave the straight and well-lit path of God's Precepts, that is when we become susceptible to the snares of the devil.

- The wicked are always working to snare and discredit the righteous. Watching the righteous fall brings comfort and delight to their souls because it gives them some measure of comparative justification. It gives them the evidence they are looking for to justify their wicked deeds. They can now say, "See, I am not so bad; no one does this correctly." But the fact of the matter is, Jesus did "this" correctly. Jesus <u>never</u> compromised. Jesus <u>never</u> strayed from the well-lit straight path of the Precepts of YHWH. Jesus, by His desire for, and consistent conformance to, the Precepts of YHWH, shines a piercingly bright light on all the compromises and wicked deeds of fallen men (and women).

  Because Jesus had laid aside His God powers (Philippians 2:5-8), and lived His incarnate life as a man (as the second Adam), because Jesus lived all of His life as a completely ordinary human being (which was an unwavering condition of His incarnation), then the testimony of His faithfulness stands as a repudiation of the proposition of Satan; it stands as a testimony of the reasonableness of walking in conformance to the Precepts of YHWH; and it stands, by its contrast to the compromises of the wicked, as the condemnation of their choices to compromise.

  This is why Jesus Christ is so hated by the wicked—it is because He legitimately robs them of all claim to any comparative justification for the compromising choices they have made. Because of the testimony of the righteous life of the second Adam, "little white lies" are now clearly seen as horrendously grievous violations of the holiness of God, and "just a little bending of the rules" are now clearly seen as unjustifiable affronts to the gracious, righteous provisions of a loving God that come to us through His Precepts. Hence, the notion of relative morality is now clearly seen for the sham that it is.

- For those who are not in Christ, this testimony of Jesus is death to them; but to those of us who <u>are</u> in Christ, this testimony of Jesus is now ours. God now sees those of us who are washed by the blood of Christ as standing above any such condemnation (Romans 8:1). The fact that Jesus, as a completely normal man, completely and consistently walked in accordance with the Precepts of YHWH, <u>is</u> the justification for those of us who are in Christ and it frees us to not be in bondage to the darkness of compromise, (so that we are no longer compelled to run and hide from the holiness of God as Adam and Eve did in Genesis 3:8, because we are no longer condemned). But instead, we are now free to run into the Light and to consistently walk in accordance with the Precepts of YHWH because that is where Jesus is. But for all this to work for us, it is critical to realize and remember that we who are in Christ are <u>not</u> justified because we walk in the light of Jesus' ways; but instead, we walk in the light of Jesus' ways because we are already completely justified before we even begin to walk in His ways. Our justification does not come from what we do and the choices we make; our justification comes <u>only</u> from what Jesus did and the choices He made. Praise be to God!

Question for you: In the above paragraph, what is the reason given for why we would want to "consistently walk in accordance to the Precepts of YHWH"?

111. "Your statutes are my heritage forever,
[for] they are the joy of my heart." (NIV)

Hebrew Literal: "<u>I have inherited</u>   <u>your testimonies</u>   <u>forever</u>
<u>for</u>   <u>the joy</u>   <u>of my heart</u>   <u>they [are]</u>."

Meditations and commentary:

- In the Hebrew, the word "for" appears explicitly at the beginning of the second line (i.e.— "for they are the joy of my heart"). This indicates a causal relationship. So, this verse can be translated as: "Because your statutes are the joy of my heart, they have become my inheritance forever."

- The Statutes of YHWH are the joy of Jesus' heart. What gives Jesus joy? The Statutes of YHWH. Where does Jesus' joy come from? The Statutes of YHWH. Satan proposed to Adam and Eve that they cut themselves off from the notion that "good" comes from being in conformance with the Statutes of YHWH. The Statutes of YHWH tell us what is good. Our fallen nature is to reject the testimonies of what God says is good in favor of what we ourselves determine to be good. Because the Statutes of YHWH proceed from, and are a reflection of, the very person of YHWH, then the rejection of the Statutes of YHWH is tantamount to the rejection of YHWH Himself. This places us in the predicament of not being able to find the satisfaction of our soul's need for joy in the infinite person of YHWH as expressed to us in His Statutes. Instead, we are relegated to the hopelessness of having no alternative but to seek the satisfaction of our soul's need for joy in the limited resources of the physical world around us. In other words, because of our fallen nature (because we have rejected the testimonies of what YHWH has said is good) we are trapped in this unfulfilling downward spiral of trying to get joy from circumstances that seem favorable to us in this physical world. And when our sense of joy comes from this physical world, our heart attaches to this physical world, and this physical world becomes our inheritance (which, by the way, cannot last).

- But for Jesus, His joy came from the Statutes of YHWH, because the Statutes of YHWH reflect the very person and character of YHWH. Jesus was in love with YHWH, therefore He was in love with the Statutes of YHWH. And because His joy needs were satisfied by the Statutes of YHWH, then by the gracious goodness of YHWH, those Statutes (indeed **YHWH Himself**) would be given to Jesus as His inheritance.

Question for you: Is it possible to love God and not love His Laws?

112. "My heart is set on keeping your decrees
    to the very end." (NIV)

Hebrew Literal: "<u>I have inclined</u>   <u>my heart</u>   <u>to perform</u>   <u>your statutes</u>
    <u>always</u>   <u>to the very end</u>."

Meditations and commentary:

- To the very end of what? Maybe this means to the very end of His life? Or maybe it means to the very end of time? In the Hebrew, the phrase, "to the very end" is preceded by the word "always." A more literal translation of this verse is: "My heart is inclined to perform your statutes always to the very end." The word "always" suggests there is an ongoing "very end." In that case, the "very end" may refer to the full and complete application of each decree. And since I suspect the numbers and types of applications for each decree are infinite, this would be a never ending, increasing familiarization and experiential intimacy with each decree. And Jesus would be saying here, then, that the <u>joy of His heart</u> (continuing the thought from v. 111) <u>will continue to increase without limit</u> as He learns and experiences all the richness of the person of YHWH as He reveals His infinite Self in His infinitely applicable decrees. (Doesn't that just blow your mind?!)

Question for you: Is it possible that, even in heaven, Jesus is engaged in a never ending process of continually increasing His experiential intimacy with His Father?

ּ Samekh (60) – Theme: Besides You and Your Law, YHWH, there is no other way to live, and on Your Law exclusively do I depend.

113. "I hate double-minded men,
      but I love your law." (NIV)

   Hebrew Literal: "Divided-mind   I hate
                    but your law   do I love."

   Meditations and commentary:

   - The Hebrew says: "I hate the divided-mind, but I love Your Law." The Hebrew is not specific about whether Christ hates divided-mindedness or divided-minded people. My inclination, based on the content of the rest of Psalm 119, is to lean toward the interpretation that Jesus is expressing how much His heart and mind do not align with those whose hearts and minds are only half-way (part-way) committed to the Law of YHWH. For Jesus, the Law of YHWH is His all-consuming passion and He has no affinity for a desire that serves two masters – God and selfish worldliness (see Matthew 6:24).

   - This entire octet seems to be focused on the need to keep separated from those who are not singly devoted to the Word and ways of YHWH. Specifically, v. 115 talks about keeping separated from evil doers; v. 118 talks about YHWH abandoning those who stray from His Decrees; and v. 119 says that YHWH discards the wicked.

   Question for you: I, and every other person who is in Christ, is a double-minded person—at least in this life. But Jesus does not hate me; in fact, it is quite the opposite. How do you explain the fact that Jesus hates double-mindedness, but He loves me (and you)?

114. "You are my refuge and my shield;
      I have put my hope in your word." (NIV)

   Hebrew Literal: "My hiding place   and my shield you   are
                    in your word   I hope."

Meditations and commentary:

- When the world is against you and the powerful people of the world rise up against you and oppose you both publicly and behind the scenes, and they exert their influence to pull the rug out from underneath you and knock down all your props—when they poison your social networks so no one wants to be associated with you anymore, when they coordinate their social and legal networks to oppress you and destroy your livelihood; when all this comes against you (and it all came against Jesus), where do you turn for refuge and protection? Jesus knew He would find refuge and protection in the word of YHWH, and that is where He focused His hope.

- I think that Jesus had so much solid hope in the word of YHWH, that when the entire world's power structure came against Him, it didn't rattle His cage because He had something that was more powerful than all the forces of this world—He had the word of YHWH. The word of YHWH provided Him with the wisdom, and counsel, and direction and authority He needed to give an answer to all those worldly powers. And it was an answer that stopped them dead in their tracks. All the world had was only Goliath, but Jesus had David's sling and stones and Jesus knew His weapons were more powerful and would prevail.

Question for you: Why and how does the word of God stop the world's most powerful people "dead in their tracks"?

115. "Away from me, you evildoers,
     that I may keep the commands of my God!" (NIV)

Hebrew Literal: "Depart   from me   evildoers
                    for I will keep   the commands   of my God."

Meditations and commentary:

- 1 Corinthians 15:33 reminds us that coordinating and cooperating with evildoers will corrupt our ways. Jesus knows this and He does not want anything to do with those who would influence Him to not keep the Commands of His God.

- Some people strongly believe (and they have degrees and certifications to reinforce this) that solutions to our life's problems can be found in all sorts of ways based on using knowledge that comes from observation and inference. That knowledge is then used to direct our disciplined efforts to effect working solutions. Jesus calls these hard-working knowledgeable "problem solvers" evildoers. In contradiction to the solutions that come from their best thinking and their best efforts, Jesus seeks solutions in the wisdom imbedded in the Commands of YHWH.

- Again, He is establishing by contrast a repudiation of the proposal Satan brought to Eve in Genesis 3. Real solutions to our lives' biggest (and smallest) problems are found in keeping the Commands of God. They are NOT found in working hard at applying the knowledge we discover from our observation and inference.

- Jesus knows that these two very different approaches (to solving life's problems) stand in opposition to each other. Each one poisons and puts to death the other, so Jesus is rejecting, dismissing, and banishing those who would encourage Him to find solutions to life's problems from anything other than the Commands of YHWH.

Question for you: Have you ever noticed that when wicked people implement solutions that align with the Commands of God, that it works out well for them? And when Christians implement solutions that do not align with the Commands of God, that those solutions do not work in the long run?

116. "Sustain me according to your promise,
    and I will live; do not let my hopes be dashed." (NIV)

Hebrew Literal: "<u>Uphold me   according to your spoken word
            and I may live   and let me not   do be ashamed   of my hope</u>."

Meditations and commentary:

- This passage can be a little difficult to translate from the Hebrew. The last line is probably more accurately translated as something like: "Do not let Me be ashamed of My hope." This has a different meaning and focus from the NIV translation. Jesus is praying here about His attitude as opposed to the steadfastness of His hope. His hope is in the Promises of God and Jesus knows that is a solid, immovable, never-failing hope. YHWH will always keep His Promises, so the hope is not in question here. But sometimes when we publicly hold onto the Promises of God, we are publicly ridiculed. Since the clinging to the Promises of God's spoken word is opposed to our fallen nature, those who are ruled by their fallen nature (which would be most people) will find it incongruous to cling to God's Promises when it appears those Promises go against common sense born from experience and our reasoning about our observations. Satan's proposition to Adam and Eve was that we should decide what is good (what makes sense) from our perspective (based on the inferences we make from our observations). So according to Satan, when a Promise of God does not seem to align with our experiences and our best thinking, then we should trust more in our best thinking and experiences than we do in the Promises of God's Word. Jesus is praying here that when the world mocks Him for clinging "irrationally" to YHWH's Promises, that mocking will not result in Jesus being less publicly bold about His trust in the Promises from YHWH's word. Jesus is asking His Father to hold Him up when this public onslaught comes so He (Jesus) will continue to exhibit a strong public testimony in favor of YHWH's Promises and in repudiation of Satan's proposition.

Question for you: The point in Jesus' life when He was most publicly humiliated and shamed was when He was stripped naked, beaten, and crucified in the company of known criminals. Why then do we now publicly and proudly display crosses as adorning jewelry?

117. "Uphold me, and I will be delivered;
       I will always have regard for your decrees." (NIV)

Hebrew Literal: "Hold me up   and I shall be safe
                and I will have regard   for your statutes   continually."

Meditations and commentary:

- For Jesus, faith is not how hard He believes, but it is knowing how active YHWH is in fulfilling what He has promised in His word. Here Jesus is recognizing that His deliverance is not based on how much Jesus can self-generate trust in YHWH's word, but His deliverance is based on the ability and willingness of YHWH to powerfully act according to His Decrees. V. 117 is not so much a plea for help as it is a celebratory praise of YHWH's faithfulness to act according to His Decrees.

Question for you: Have you come to the point, yet, where you realize that your faith is not effective because of how hard you believe, but it is effective because of how powerful and faithful God is to do what He has promised?

118. "You reject all who stray from your decrees,
    for their deceitfulness is in vain." (NIV)

Hebrew Literal: "Have trodden down   all   those who stray
            from your statutes
        for   [is] falsehood   their deceit."

Meditations and commentary:

- "Trodden down" (the literal Hebrew) has a different connotation than "reject." God is active and relentless to cause those who oppose His ways to be unsuccessful. They will be unsuccessful because they have attempted to implement solutions that ultimately do not work. Those solutions are based on a wrong understanding of how God works and therefore how life works. If God were to cause them to be ultimately successful, then He would be working in opposition to Himself.

- This does not mean that God would not allow apparent initial success to come about for those who stray from God's ways, but these apparent initial successes will ultimately result in emptiness in the souls of those who achieve those deceitful successes.

    Question for you: Have you ever gotten something you really wanted and worked hard for, only to have it end up not being very satisfying in the end? Is that because it was not aligned with the Statutes of God?

119. "All the wicked of the earth you discard like dross;
    therefore I love your statutes." (NIV)

Hebrew Literal: "[Like] dross you   put away   the all   wicked
            of the earth
        therefore   I love   your testimonies."

Meditations and commentary:

- Continuing on from the commentary from the previous verse (v. 118), those who pursue success based on something that contradicts the Statutes of YHWH end up in only futility. This truth leads Jesus to love and be devoted to the Statutes of YHWH. Jesus is not interested in embracing the futility of deceitfulness; He is therefore, very interested in conducting His life in accordance with the Statutes of YHWH.

Question for you: Have you ever viewed the Statutes of God as predictors of success?

120. "My flesh trembles in fear of you;
      I stand in awe of your laws." (NIV)

Hebrew Literal: "Trembles   for fear   my flesh
                and of your judgments   I am afraid."

Meditations and commentary:

- Jesus recognizes that not only are the Laws of YHWH powerful and effective in upholding Him and delivering Him and sustaining Him and protecting Him, but the Laws of YHWH are the only way to His being upheld (v. 117) and delivered (v. 117) and sustained (v. 116) and protected (v. 114). The very thought of not being in complete alignment with the Laws of YHWH causes Jesus to shudder. For Jesus, the thought of not being fully aligned with the Laws of YHWH is so full of horror that it causes Him to be very troubled about anything that would influence Him to violate the Laws of YHWH. All of this fear ultimately proceeds from the extreme regard Jesus has for the holiness of YHWH – which Jesus sees reflected in the Laws of YHWH.

- Lord Jesus, I stand in awe of Your high regard for, and unwavering commitment and faithfulness to, the Laws of YHWH! Certainly, You are worthy of our praise! You are worthy of all the honor we could possibly acknowledge! You are the righteous One!

Question for you: Does it frighten you to think about doing something in your life that does not align with the Laws of God as they are written in Scripture?

ע **Ayin (70)** – Theme: Therefore, I esteem Your Precepts to be right; they apply to everything. Any other proposed solution is false and I hate it.

121. "I have done what is righteous and just;
        do not leave me to my oppressors." (NIV)

      Hebrew Literal: "I have done   judgment   and justice
                        not   do leave me   to my oppressors."

Meditations and commentary:

- In the light of Romans 3:10-18,20 this is a statement that could only be made by Jesus Christ.

- It would be delusional for any of the rest of us to claim God's deliverance based on our own righteousness. Any claim we make based on our own righteousness before YHWH will not turn out well for us.

- And what deliverance is Jesus claiming? That He should not be left to His oppressors. Which oppressors? That is answered for us in the next verse (v. 122). The arrogant.

Question for you: What does it mean to be arrogant?

122. "Ensure your servant's well-being;
        let not the arrogant oppress me." (NIV)

      Hebrew Literal: "Be a pledge   for your servant   for good
                        not   do let oppress me   the proud."

Meditations and commentary:

- This verse is an elaboration of the second line of the previous verse (v. 121).

- Who are the arrogant? Arrogance, in the context of Psalm 119, is the belief that there is a way to be right apart from being perfectly aligned with the Law of YHWH. Again, this arrogance is Satan's proposition—that we can determine the correct course of action in a situation apart from the revealed word of God. The arrogant have a crucial vested interest in seeing that Jesus' proposition fails. Jesus' proposition is that only relying on YHWH as He leads us through His Statutes, Testimonies, Promises, and Laws will result in a life lived rightly. No other path will work.

On the other hand, the arrogant, in conformance with Satan's proposition to Adam and Eve, are in pursuit of a righteousness that supposedly comes from doing one's best to do good. The belief that it is appropriate to live life by doing one's best to do good <u>is</u> the height of arrogance. It is a futile attempt on our part to be like God—by our deciding what is good. Jesus is praying here for the repudiation of that whole approach to life; He is praying that the futility of that approach will publicly be seen as the sham that it is, and that those who oppose His approach will be publicly defanged.

Question for you: Do you see that if you believe that "doing your best to do good will be acceptable to God," then you are one of the arrogant; you are delusional; and you justly deserve the coming wrath of God—unless you change your thinking about how you become acceptable to God (because it is certainly not by doing your best to do good)?

123. "My eyes fail, looking for your salvation,
     looking for your righteous promise." (NIV)

    Hebrew Literal: "<u>My eyes</u>   <u>strain</u>   <u>for your salvation</u>
                 <u>for the spoken word</u>   <u>of your righteousness</u>."

  AND

124. "Deal with your servant according to your love
     and teach me your decrees." (NIV)

    Hebrew Literal: "<u>Deal</u>   <u>with</u>   <u>your servant</u>
                 <u>according to your covenant loyalty</u>
                 <u>and your statutes</u>   <u>teach me</u>."

Meditations and commentary:

- As we have said in earlier commentary in this book, the scope of the application and insights of God's Laws and Promises are infinite (because they proceed from and reflect His Person which is infinite). As humans, we have finite faculties (finite minds, limited time, finite perspective, etc.). It is an impossible task for a finite person to properly grasp and apply the infinite wealth of the wisdom of God as revealed through His Promises and Decrees. The only hope the incarnate Jesus could have of doing this properly was for His Father to continually show Him which Promises and Decrees to apply in what ways to each particular aspect of every different situation He faced. I think when Jesus says that His eyes "strain" looking for the right Promise to apply in the right way, He is saying that He is not equipped in His incarnate form to do this, and therefore He needs YHWH to show Him what Decree gets applied where, every moment of every day, in accordance with the eternal covenant love the Father has for Him.

- Only if YHWH will be faithful to Jesus in this way, will Jesus be able to live in accordance with the responsibilities and obligations that appear in the previous two verses (vv. 121 and 122).

- Again, here we see that Jesus has no desire or intent to solve life's puzzles as best He can, but instead, He continually relies on the provision of YHWH. This, again, is a contrast between Satan's proposition (as it appears in Genesis 3) and the proposition of God (as it appears in Genesis 1 and 2). (And I am willing to bet that Jesus' I.Q. was much higher than mine or yours.)

Question for you: How would your life be different if you began to refuse to solve life's puzzles as best you could, but instead, continually relied only on God's provisions as the Holy Spirit reveals them to you when you read His word?

125. "I am your servant; give me discernment
     that I may understand your statutes." (NIV)

Hebrew Literal: "Your servant   I am   give me understanding
                    that I may know   your testimonies."

Meditations and commentary:

- Following the theme discussed in the previous verses (vv. 121-124), Jesus is wanting to understand YHWH's Statutes, but He is acknowledging two things in this quest:

- The understanding will come because YHWH gives Him discernment, not because Jesus figures it out on His own; and
- As YHWH's servant, Jesus is appealing to the obligation that YHWH has to provide this discernment. YHWH is so obligated because He has sent Jesus, as His servant, to carry out this mission, and it is the obligation of the master who sends, to also provide the resources necessary to make the mission successful. Employers do not send employees on business trips without also providing the travel, lodging, and meal money necessary for the trip to be successful.

Question for you: Does it seem to you that experientially knowing the Testimonies and Statutes of God is a good way to get to experientially know God Himself?

126. "It is time for you to act, YHWH;
     your law is being broken." (NIV)

Hebrew Literal: "[It is] time for   to act   YHWH
                 [for] they have broken   your law."

Meditations and commentary:

- When God the Son prays to God the Father with an injunction for immediate action, what do you think will happen? In Hebrews 1:8, the Father calls the Son His (the Father's) God. Do you think God the Father will do as God the Son asks? All of eternity would unravel if He did not. This voice was the same one with the authority to speak the cosmos into existence. This same voice is now requiring YHWH to act. Do you think YHWH will act, and act immediately? Nothing could be more certain!

- So, this begs the question: "What action is being requested here?" What is the appropriate response of YHWH to the fact that His Law has been broken? This could get real scary real fast. What is the appropriate response of the thrice Holy, all powerful, all seeing, always present sovereign Ruler of all that is, to the fact that His Law is being broken?

- Satan's argument is that the reasonable response is to eradicate the offender. That is the judgment that Satan proposes—and that is the judgment that a vast host of sentient beings expected. But obviously, that is not the Divine action Jesus was asking for or none of us would be here to ponder this (although that

Behold the Christ   Copyright © 2018, Richard L. Routh, All rights reserved.

would have been a just action).

- What is God's response to sin? What is God's response to His Law being broken? Well, history is clear on the answer to this question. YHWH's response to the violation of His holiness is to pour out His wrath on His Son as the just substitutionary payment for our violation of His holiness when we ignore His Law. God's response is to show us mercy by judging His Son in our place. History is clear on this. So, ultimately, that is the action YHWH takes in response to His Law being broken. But is that what is being requested here? Is Jesus asking in v. 126 for YHWH to immediately have His Son be crucified? Unless Jesus only prayed this verse in the Garden of Gethsemane on the night before His crucifixion (which He may well also have done), then Jesus was asking for some other "immediate" action in this verse.

  What action then was Jesus requesting of His Father as the appropriate immediate response to YHWH's law being broken? The context of this octet gives us the answer to that question. And now the college professor in me rears its head and says, "Let's see if you have been properly following the discussion. So, I leave it as an exercise for the student to answer this question. (It is an important answer.)"

Question for you: What action was Jesus requesting of His Father as the appropriate immediate response to YHWH's Law being broken?

127. "Because I love your commands more than gold,
  more than pure gold," (NIV)

  Hebrew Literal: "<u>Therefore</u>   <u>thus</u>   <u>I love</u>   <u>your commands</u>
        <u>more than gold</u>   <u>even pure gold</u>."

Meditations and commentary:

- If you came up with the right answer to the question I asked at the end of the commentary of the previous verse (v. 126), then you will know why vv. 127 and 128 follow v. 126. Well, let's talk about it.

- This verse begins with the word "therefore" (in the Hebrew) which means that it logically follows from the previous verse.

- Because the Divine will of YHWH is to have mercy on, and provide righteousness for, sinful people, He has therefore equipped the Christ with all the discernment He needed to properly demonstrate the repudiation of Satan's proposition.

- Because of YHWH's mercy and provision, because it is in the person and character of YHWH to have mercy on the elect, Jesus loved the means by which that mercy and provision came: namely, through His keeping the Commands of YHWH. And therefore, Jesus elevated (esteemed) the value of those Commands to be greater (because they were more efficaciously powerful) than the most valuable material wealth that the fallen world could offer (which was, at that time in history, commonly viewed to be lots of pure gold).

- Jesus was reveling in, rejoicing and celebrating, the surpassingly great mercy and provision of YHWH as He showers it on the elect. And that He does that through the giving to the Christ, via YHWH's commands, the discernment and understanding Jesus needed to properly complete His redemptive mission.

- At this point in the reader's progress through this book, **it should be evident that one of the greatest understatements of all time was when Jesus said in Matthew 5:17, "Do not think that I have come to abolish the law or the prophets; I have not come to abolish them but to fulfill them."**

Question for you: What else did Jesus say about this—what do the next two verses say that follow Matthew 5:17?

128. "and because I consider all your precepts right,
     I hate every wrong path." (NIV)

Hebrew Literal: "<u>Therefore</u>   <u>thus</u>   <u>all</u>   <u>[your] precepts</u>
              <u>concerning everything</u>   <u>I esteem right</u>
              <u>every</u>   <u>way</u>   <u>false</u>   <u>I hate</u>."

Meditations and commentary:

- The structure of the NIV translation of this verse tends to suggest that the second line is the theme of the verse. However, if the Hebrew is translated more in accordance with the traditional practices of translation, then this verse might be translated into English as: "And therefore I consider all Your Precepts in the way they concern everything [all the little details of everything] to be right, [and/so] I hate every wrong path." This suggests Jesus saw "hating every wrong path" to be a corollary to "considering all Your Precepts, concerning everything, to be right." Therefore, the theme and focus of this verse would not be "hating every wrong path" but the theme and focus would be on the fact that all the Precepts of YHWH have something quintessentially definitional to say about <u>every</u> little detail of everything. In other words, nothing in all of creation, no matter how big or small, is outside the scope of the Precepts of YHWH. This notion of the universal scope of the Precepts of YHWH leaves no room for anything that might consider the possibility of something being able to operate apart from (beyond, independent of) the Precepts of YHWH. And anything to suggest otherwise is wrong and is to be rejected out of hand. Specifically, the thing that is wrong is Satan's proposition that OUR judgments about right and wrong could be legitimate when they are independent of the Precepts dictated by YHWH.

Question for you: If John 17:3 means that the only thing that really matters is getting to experientially know God and Jesus Christ whom He has sent, then why would you even want to ever consider anything apart from the Precepts of God?

Behold the Christ   Copyright © 2018, Richard L. Routh, All rights reserved.

פ **Pe (80)** – Theme: Because You love Me, give Your greatest blessing to Me by teaching Me Your Statutes.

129. "Your statutes are wonderful;
    therefore I obey them." (NIV)

    Hebrew Literal: "[Are] wonderful   your testimonies
                    therefore   thus   does keep them   my soul."

    Meditations and commentary:

    • The Hebrew word palaowt (translated here as "wonderful") is a form of the Hebrew word pele which is translated as "a wonder," or as "astonishing," or as "wonderful." It derives from the Hebrew word pala which means miracle. So, this verse might be translated as: "Your Statutes are astonishingly miraculous and therefore I keep (guard) them."

    • Jesus, in His incarnate form, never quits being Himself. That is to say, He never quits being God. Yes, He laid aside His God-powers per Philippians 2, but He never laid aside His identity as God. Therefore, whatever Jesus did has divine importance because it has the focus, and therefore the attributed value, of the eternal Divine intent.

    • Conversely, Jesus had the Divine obligation (responsibility) to only pay attention to, and keep or guard, those things that are worthy of the eternal Divine attention. (Because, after all, anything He paid attention to was by definition worthy of His eternal Divine attention.) In this regard, Jesus is saying here in v. 129, that the Statutes of YHWH are worthy of that eternal Divine attention because they are that valuable as testified to by their astonishingly miraculous wonder.

    Question for you: If you are in Christ, does that have any implication on the importance of the things you focus your attention on? (See Romans 6 for more discussion on this thought.)

130. "The unfolding of your words gives light;
    it gives understanding to the simple." (NIV)

Hebrew Literal: "The unfolding   of your words   gives light
                 it gives understanding to   the simple."

Meditations and commentary:

- So, does Jesus consider Himself to be a simple person? In His incarnate form is He simple-minded? The book of Proverbs claims that one of its purposes is to give prudence (wisdom) to the simple (Proverbs 1:4). We know from Luke 2:52 that Jesus grew (advanced) in wisdom. He no doubt turned in part to the book of Proverbs for that wisdom.

- The word "unfolding" conveys a step-by-step process. The further one goes in this process, the more light one gets.

- Jesus saw that His incarnate mind was too simple to have the understanding He needed to make the wise decisions He was supposed to be making. He turned to the word of YHWH and expected YHWH to unfold it through a continual process of reading, prayer, meditation, revelation and practice. Through this process of unfolding the word of YHWH, Jesus received the light of understanding He needed to make the wise decisions He was supposed to be making.

Question for you: Is it possible to be wise apart from the spoken word of YHWH as it is written in the Scriptures and unfolded to us by the Holy Spirit?

131. "I open my mouth and pant,
         longing for your commands." (NIV)

      Hebrew Literal: "My mouth   I opened   and panted
                        for   your commands   I longed."

Meditations and commentary:

- In humans, panting is a physiological means of increasing oxygen to the muscles so that vigorous exercise can continue. Perhaps Jesus is painting a picture here of vigorously pursuing putting the Commands of YHWH into action in His life. For Him it is a continuous exercise, and one He seeks to accelerate.

- The attitude of our "natural man" is to shun and run from the Commands of God. Our fallen nature says, "No thanks, God. I can do this by myself. I will figure it out." But Jesus is showing us here that His attitude is to run toward and enthusiastically embrace the Commands of YHWH. This contrast is a quintessential difference between our fallen nature and our regenerate nature. It was a mark of distinction of Jesus' nature. It is the contrast between reliance on the provision of God vs. independence from God and His provision in favor of reliance on our own knowledge and efforts.

Question for you: Some people think that "walking in the Spirit" is the same thing as, or at least is indistinguishable from, having a strong *affinity* for the Testimonies of YHWH as recorded in Scripture. What do you think about this?

132. "Turn to me and have mercy on me,
      as you always do to those who love your name." (NIV)

Hebrew Literal: "<u>Look you</u>   <u>on me</u>   <u>and be merciful</u>
                 <u>after your manner</u>   <u>with those who love</u>   <u>your name</u>."

Meditations and commentary:

- In v. 121 of the previous octet, Jesus pleads for YHWH's provision on the basis of the merit of His own obedience and His own righteousness, as only He can. Here, Jesus is asking for YHWH's provision on the basis of the character of YHWH, specifically His character of mercy.

- Our Father in heaven is merciful with those who love His name. (But none of loves God until we see His mercy.) God is the initiator. Mercy is His idea. Mercy is what happens when He reveals Himself to us. Mercy is when the unapproachable, thrice Holy, Lord, God almighty (Revelation 4:8) chooses to share Himself with us (John 17:20-21) and to grant us experiential knowledge of Himself, which is what eternal life is (John 17:3).

- It would not be possible for a human person, with our relative extreme limitations, to know, let alone even approach, the infinite Holy God, unless God gives an infinite measure of mercy to us—even to the extent of bidding us to <u>boldly</u> approach His throne (Hebrews 4:16).

- Jesus is appealing to this character of mercy in YHWH to be the provision that bridges the gap between the finiteness of incarnation and the infinite Holiness and power of YHWH. It is a way in which the Son worships the Father—that is to recognize and rely upon the nature of YHWH to extend extreme mercy to Him (and us).

Question for you: Have you ever considered it an act of divine mercy when God allows you to read His word?

133. "Direct my footsteps according to your word;
      let no sin rule over me." (NIV)

Hebrew Literal: "<u>My steps</u>   <u>order</u>   <u>by your spoken word</u>
                        <u>and not</u>   <u>do let have dominion</u>   <u>in me</u>   <u>any</u>   <u>iniquity</u>."

Meditations and commentary:

- Continuing on in the theme of v. 132, one of the ways in which YHWH shows the incarnate Christ mercy (and shows us mercy, too) is to direct Jesus' (and our) actions in accordance with YHWH's word—and preventing any iniquity from taking hold in Jesus' life. Again we see that for Christ to live a righteous life, it requires a partnership between Him and the provision of the Almighty Holy YHWH. Jesus has His role to fulfill (namely to be dependent on the provision of YHWH) and YHWH has His role to fulfill (namely to mercifully provide everything the Christ needs to live a righteous life). This is accomplished by ordering Jesus' steps with the Commands and Precepts in the word of YHWH.

- What is iniquity? Apparently it is what takes dominion in you whenever your steps are not ordered by the word of God. It is contrary to the word of God. It is the knowledge and counsel of people who do "their" best to do good. It is the alternate path we walk down when we reject (ignore) the counsels of the word of God. It is what happens when people think they can figure out on their own what good looks like. I.e.—it is the full embracing of Satan's proposition to Eve in Genesis 3:1-7.

Question for you: Do you yet realize that "doing your best to do good" is the height of rebellion against God? How does "doing your best to do good" fit into Genesis 3:1-7?

        Copyright © 2018, Richard L. Routh, All rights reserved.

134. "Redeem me from the oppression of men,
      that I may obey your precepts." (NIV)

Hebrew Literal: "<u>Deliver me</u>   <u>from the oppression</u>   <u>of man</u>
                  <u>so will I keep</u>   <u>your precepts</u>."

Meditations and commentary:

- What is "the oppression of men"? Jesus is asking YHWH to deliver Him from the oppression of men. From the text, evidently, "the oppression of men" is contrary to keeping the Precepts of YHWH. People are oppressed in their souls, and oppress others, when they choose a path apart from keeping the Precepts of YHWH. Because we are created in the image of God, our souls can be satisfied only by God Himself. Even for us believers, when we choose to reject God (in some area of our lives) by rejecting His revelation of Himself to us through His word (in that area), when we in essence say, "I don't need to know what the Bible says because I can figure out what is good on my own," then a portion of our souls are filled with darkness. God is the initiator and provider of life and all that is good for us. When we reject His provision through the revelation of Himself through His spoken word, there is nothing left for us but to stumble around in an empty darkness. But because we choose to justify ourselves, we call this stumbling in empty darkness "being enlightened." (A trick we learned from our father the devil who convinced us it is better to stumble in empty darkness than it is to walk in the light of YHWH's word.) This empty darkness is "the oppression of men."

- But how are we sinners supposed to respond? We might want to consider Romans 2:4, which says, "Or do you show contempt for the riches of his kindness, forbearance and patience, not realizing that God's kindness is intended to lead you to repentance?"

Question for you: Have you ever felt oppressed? Have you ever thought that this could be caused by being functionally disconnected from the word of God?

135. "Make your face shine upon your servant
      and teach me your decrees." (NIV)

Hebrew Literal: "<u>Make your face</u>   <u>to shine</u>   <u>upon your servant</u>
                  <u>and teach</u>   <u>me</u>   <u>your statutes</u>."

Meditations and commentary:

- (continuing on from the commentary for v. 134) The empty darkness that comes from ignoring the Decrees of YHWH stands in stark contrast to the light of God's Person that floods our soul. This is what the Hebrew idiom means: "May Your face shine upon me." Learning the Decrees of YHWH (as spoken by Him in the Scriptures) is what produces that light in our souls. But learning the Decrees of YHWH is not something that can be done apart from God revealing their meaning and application to us. Hence, Jesus' request for YHWH to teach Him His Decrees.

Question for you: Do you want more light in your life? According to this verse, where do you go to get it?

136. "Streams of tears flow from my eyes,
    for your law is not obeyed." (NIV)

Hebrew Literal: "<u>Rivers</u> <u>of water</u> <u>run down</u> <u>my eyes</u>
    <u>because</u> <u>not</u> <u>do do they keep</u> <u>your law</u>."

Meditations and commentary:

- When you first come across something that is good, you want to share it with others you care about. When I first discovered Godiva chocolate truffles, I wanted to share them with everyone in my family. It thrilled my soul to be the one who could thrill the souls of people I cared about with this great new taste sensation. If you were suffering from pneumonia in a hospital ward where people all around you were dying daily from pneumonia and you just found out about penicillin, wouldn't you want to share that miraculous discovery with everyone on that ward—knowing that penicillin would cure them all and rescue them from much suffering and death? Or imagine you lived in a community of diabetics when insulin treatments were first discovered. Wouldn't you be driven to let everyone else know about this wonderful new treatment to alleviate their suffering? And if those you cared about did not believe what you had to say about the delightful taste of Godiva truffles or the healing power of penicillin or insulin, would this not cause you great sorrow? Would this not cause you to weep and mourn as you watched those suffer and die when you know you have the cure? Well, this is just like what Jesus is sorrowful about in this verse. He knows first-hand the extreme benefits that come to a soul who cherishes and keeps the Law of God, but He is surrounded by those He loves who do not believe Him when He tells them about the great blessings that will be theirs if they, too, love and keep the Law of God. When He sees those He cares about rejecting the love and provision of YHWH that comes through His Law, it causes Him great sorrow.

- But we know that because of our broken minds and desires, when we get close to the Law of God, it kills/condemns us (if we try to use it as a means to increase our righteousness or our approval from God; or when we think our obedience of the Law of God makes us better Christians). Because of this, we are unwilling (and unable) to keep the Law of YHWH. With this realization, Jesus' desire to bless us with the goodness of the Law of YHWH is not thwarted because it is at this point that Jesus committed Himself to keep the Law for us and then, at His death, exchange His righteousness for our sin.

- Praise be to Jesus our Redeemer and King who has seen to it that by His efforts we will have the full blessings of One who has fully kept the Law of YHWH. This is how grace comes to us through the Law of YHWH—Jesus did it all for us!

Question for you: Do you ever feel like keeping the Law of God is a burden? If so, according to the above commentary, what two things are you failing to accept that causes you to feel that burden?

Copyright © 2018, Richard L. Routh, All rights reserved.

צ **Tsadhe (90)** – Theme: You and Your goodness, YHWH, are inseparable from the Judgments of Your Law, and in this do I delight.

137. "Righteous are you, YHWH,
    and your laws are right." (NIV)

    Hebrew Literal: "<u>Righteous are you YHWH</u>
            <u>and upright [are] your judgments</u>."

    Meditations and commentary:

    - In a world where Jesus felt like a stranger, where He was surrounded by voices and relationships that continually oppressed Him, where streams of tears flowed from His eyes because of the sin and futility He saw every time He opened them—in that world Jesus' only point of sanity and hope, and the only place where He could look to see something that was right, was the Law of YHWH.

    - This verse is a cry of relief. It is a celebration of what is right in the midst of so much else that is wrong. It is a rejoicing in the refuge and strength that comes from the sanity of the Laws of YHWH in a world filled with insanity. It is a prayer of thankfulness. It is a prayer of praise.

    Question for you: When you think about the Laws of God as contained in the Bible, have you ever wanted to celebrate and bust out in grateful praise to God for giving us something that is always right and true and good?

138. "The statutes you have laid down are righteous;
    they are fully trustworthy." (NIV)

    Hebrew Literal: "<u>[What] you have commanded [is] righteous</u>
            <u>your testimonies and faithful abundantly</u>."

    Meditations and commentary:

    - Continuing from v. 137, Jesus is exulting in the abundant faithfulness of YHWH's Testimonies/Statutes. In a world where everyone is advocating relativism, tolerance, and shifting values, Jesus finds refuge in the Commands (Testimonies) of YHWH. They never change and are always completely appropriate and applicable to every need for wise counsel, good advice, and right thinking. It was unthinkable and completely ridiculous in Jesus thinking to look anywhere other than the Commands of YHWH for answers in life. The proposition that answers could be found by people's reasoning about their observations and experiences was an ugly and foreign thought to Jesus.

- I praise You, Lord Jesus, because You are the only right minded person who ever lived. Worthy is the Lamb who was slain to receive wisdom (Revelation 5:12)!

Question for you: Are you getting the picture that Jesus really, really, REALLY loves the Commandments of YHWH?

139. "My zeal wears me out,
   for my enemies ignore your words." (NIV)

Hebrew Literal: "Has consumed me   my zeal
                 because   have forgotten   your words   my enemies."

Meditations and commentary:

- Jesus has zeal for the words of YHWH. We have certainly well established that in the previous 138 verses of this Psalm.

- Jesus' enemies ignore the words of YHWH. They may occasionally feign acknowledgement of their validity, but they never really rely on them. What they rely on are their own judgments about what is right and wrong based on their own experiences and observations, and they use those as a basis for evaluating the potential usefulness and applicability of the words of YHWH. In this way, we are continually sitting in judgment of the Law of God and we fail to let the words of YHWH stand all by themselves on the credibility and trustworthiness of God. This attitude of ours makes us Jesus' enemies. (It is only when we trust Jesus to be righteousness for us, that we reverse this curse.)

- What we are saying here is that perhaps some of His enemies might even publicly acknowledge the advisability of holding the general concept of the word of God in high esteem, but they (we) ignore the specific application of the individual Laws of God to their personal lives. In other words, they might publicly say something like, "Everyone knows the word of God is a good thing." And they might make some show of honoring the word of God such as placing their family

Bible in a place of honor in their home. But they do not often, if ever, defer to the specific Laws and Commands of God to dictate how they will make the tough decisions in their lives. That is what Jesus means when He says His enemies ignore the words of YHWH.

- When I was a kid, a respected person in authority told me, "Religion can be a good thing in your life, but you don't want to go overboard with it." By this he meant that it was a good thing to publicly acknowledge and honor God and religion, but that I should not make the mistake of using the Bible to decide what all my actions should be. This would be the type of perspective that Jesus would say characterized His enemies. This is the counsel by which Jesus' enemies actually live their personal lives.

- The entire 23rd chapter of the Gospel of Matthew (among several others) is a running list and commentary from Jesus of examples of this sort of thing.

- How did this wear Jesus out? Because it wears anyone out to push and push on a locked door trying to open it, but it remains locked. The longer one pushes, the more worn out they become.

- Jesus was constantly advocating and encouraging people to go to the word of YHWH to find the solutions to their problems, but rarely did people follow His advice. Instead, they would try to figure out the solutions by themselves.

- There is another aspect to this dynamic of Jesus being worn out (or consumed) by His zeal. The more Jesus advised people to seek their answers from the word of YHWH, the more they got tired and bothered by this incessantly dripping advice, and they began explicitly opposing Jesus by their words and actions. Responding to this constant barrage of opposition wore Jesus out.

- Praise God that Jesus has given us His Holy Spirit who continually encourages us to seek answers in the word of God! We who are in Christ experience the hope and comfort and counsel we receive when we prayerfully search God's word. This is a great gift of God's provision to us and it was won for us by the life and sacrifice of Jesus. Praise be to Jesus for providing us with His Spirit who gives us His desires!

Question for you: Do you mourn when you see those you care about ignoring the counsel of Scripture?

140. "Your promises have been thoroughly tested,
     and your servant loves them." (NIV)

Hebrew Literal: "<u>Pure</u>   <u>your spoken word</u>   <u>[is] very</u>
                  <u>therefore your servant</u>   <u>loves it</u>."

Meditations and commentary:

- Not often in this world, but occasionally, something is so good that it surpasses our expectations in very many ways. It surprises us over and over with how much better it performs in meeting our needs than we ever expected. In 2008, at the urging of some friends who were trying to improve my business image, I purchased a new car: an Infiniti G-35. I'm really not that much of a car guy. I am usually quite content to just have reliable, comfortable, affordable transportation. My friends (and business counselors) told me my penchant for inexpensive basic transportation was projecting an image of less business success than the quality of the executive consulting I was providing at the time; and that bare-bones image was inconsistent with, and damaging to, the brand perception of what I was delivering to the marketplace. So, they advised me to purchase a car that was more consistent with the brand image I was working to establish. That is why one day I found myself driving off the car lot in a brand new Infiniti G-35.

  Nearly everything about that car continued to surprise me with how excellently it was designed and built and performed. I was constantly surprised by the high-powered racing-car-like performance and handling of that car. I was constantly surprised by the many thoughtful features that constantly reminded me that I was experiencing the comfort and convenience of true luxury. I often had the feeling of being undeserving of such excellence of performance and comfort and the result was that I was constantly grateful for that car. At the risk of sounding idolatrous, that car so exceeded my expectations and I was so grateful for it, that I can say I really loved that car.

- This is the same idea being conveyed in this verse—especially in the Hebrew. At every turn, the promises of YHWH exceeded expectations in so many unexpected ways that Jesus proclaims, "Your servant loves them!" Jesus' experience was that the "spoken word" of YHWH (which came to Him in written form in the Scriptures) was so practically useful and appropriate in so many important and unexpected ways that it constantly surprised and thrilled His soul.

  I realize it is a trite comparison to show the emotional similarity between a new high-powered luxury sports car and the word of God, but I'm trying to communicate the emotional thrill, and the reasons for that thrill, that Jesus experienced when He applied the word of God to the challenges He had in His life.

- Oh, that we would allow God to surprise us with the astounding, unexpected practical usefulness of His word when it is applied in our lives! Oh, that our souls would be thrilled in the same way that Jesus' soul was thrilled by the overwhelming power, veracity, and appropriateness of the Word of God when it is applied in our lives!

Question for you: Do you think you will ever get to the point where the possession you most treasure on earth (in this life) is the word of God?

141. "Though I am lowly and despised,
  I do not forget your precepts." (NIV)

Hebrew Literal: "<u>Lowly</u>   <u>am I</u>   <u>and despised</u>
  <u>your precepts</u>   <u>not</u> <u>do I forget</u>."

Meditations and commentary:

- Jesus never quits being God. As we focus on the nature and function of His incarnation, we must never forget that this Man is the same Person who is part of the God-head. He is the same Person by whom and through whom all things were made (Colossians 1:15-17 and John 1:3). He is the same Person in whom all the fullness of YHWH dwells (Colossians 1:19). He is the same Person in whose image we are created. Although Jesus was God, and never quits being God, for His incarnation He laid aside His God powers (Philippians 2) to become a lowly and despised Man who was entirely submitted to the precepts of YHWH.

  It is the same for those of us who are in Christ. Although we are seated now with Christ in the heavenlies at the right hand of God the Father—and are thus exalted above all the rest of creation (including Satan), we have been called, for this time of our incarnation, to temporarily lay aside much of what is already ours in the heavenlies and to live our lives now, as Christ did, submitted to the Precepts of YHWH in a lowly and despised state. In this way, we are granted the extreme privilege of following our Savior and experiencing the reality of His incarnation! Certainly this is part of what it means to be created in the image of God! And we should wear it as a badge of divine honor! Jesus did.

Question for you: Does God withhold any good thing from you? How much good does He provide for you through His Precepts? How many of those good provisions has Jesus already earned for you?

142. "Your righteousness is everlasting
and your law is true." (NIV)

Hebrew Literal: "Your righteousness   [is] a righteousness   everlasting
and your law   [is] the truth."

Meditations and commentary:

- The emotional context of this verse is given in the next two verses. Jesus was troubled and in anguish and feeling like His life was in jeopardy (vv. 143 & 144). Certainly He felt this way in the Garden of Gethsemane the night before His crucifixion, but I am persuaded He felt this way continually throughout His entire earthly ministry, and perhaps even His entire life. In the midst of this emotional turmoil, Jesus drew strength and hope from the fact that YHWH's righteousness was an everlasting righteousness, and as such, it was a permanent, unwavering anchor in which Jesus could take refuge—a refuge that would not be tossed to and fro like so much of the world around Him seemed to be. And in a world where all those around Him were subscribing to values of tolerance, relativism, and appeasement, and whose favorite word seemed to be "whatever" (or whatever the first century Aramaic equivalent was), Jesus got hope and strength from the fact that YHWH's Law was the truth. YHWH's Law is a truth that <u>never</u> changes; it never bends with the pressures and influences of a people who are in the process of determining "good" for themselves; it never wavers; it is never fickle. The Law of YHWH remains eternally above all that fickleness. This fact was a great solace to Jesus.

Question for you: Do you take solace in knowing that the Laws of YHWH are unmovable, unflexing eternal statements of absolute truth?

143. "Trouble and distress have come upon me,
but your commands are my delight." (NIV)

Hebrew Literal: "<u>Trouble</u>　<u>and anguish</u>　<u>have come upon me</u>
<u>[yet] your commands [are]</u>　<u>my delight</u>."

Meditations and commentary:

- As you can see from the Hebrew literal above, the word "distress" in the NIV can also be translated as "anguish." By this point in this book we have established the causes for Jesus' anguish. Those causes, the many destructive beliefs and behaviors of the people around Jesus, for whom He cared very much, were continually oppressing Him. In the midst of this constant oppression, Jesus needed something in which He could genuinely delight. He needed something He could cling to that was the opposite of all the destructive beliefs and behaviors of the people around Him. He found this need satisfied in the Commands of YHWH.

  Question for you: What is the best way for you to respond to the fact that Jesus found great hope and delight in the Commands of YHWH?

144. "Your statutes are forever right;
     give me understanding that I may live." (NIV)

   Hebrew Literal: "<u>The righteousness</u>　<u>of your testimonies</u>　<u>[is] everlasting</u>
   <u>give me understanding</u>　<u>and I shall live</u>."

Meditations and commentary:

- Continuing from the thoughts in the previous few verses, Jesus gained the strength He needed to continue "fighting the good fight" and not quit and give up His life, from the understanding that YHWH gave Him. YHWH gave Him understanding about the righteousness of His Statutes, and that understanding is what gave Jesus the strength He needed to not give up. We do not usually recognize that a better understanding of the Statutes of YHWH gives us strength. As a matter of fact, for us, because of our sinfulness, understanding the Statutes of YHWH brings us death/condemnation (Romans 7:9-25).

- I praise You, Lord Jesus, that Your character and motivations were so pure that the Statutes of YHWH were a source of life for You, and not a source of death! And now this purity, and these desires of Yours are henceforth credited to me and my brothers and sisters! You carried this weight for us!

Question for you: If living by the Statutes and Testimonies of YHWH do not make us better Christians, and since they also do not gain us greater favor or approval in God's sight, then why should we embrace them?

ק **Qoph (100)** – Theme: I (Jesus) cried out with all My heart: save Me, YHWH, to keep Your eternal Statutes.

145. "I call with all my heart; answer me, YHWH,
      and I will obey your decrees." (NIV)

      Hebrew Literal: "I cried   with all   [my] heart   answer me   YHWH
                      your statutes   I will keep."

Meditations and commentary:

- Verses 150 and 151 give the context for this octet. Two different parties are drawing near to Jesus. Each of these two parties has an agenda that proceeds from their identity. Jesus is feeling the pressure, and it is evidently a very strong, even nearly overwhelming pressure, to conform to each party's identity. The two parties that bring this intense pressure on Jesus are: (1) those who devise wicked schemes (v. 150) and, (2) YHWH with His Commands (v. 151). The tension between these intensely pushed, and mutually exclusive, agendas are so burdensome on the soul of Christ that all of the first three verses of this octet (vv. 145, 146, and 147) are exclamations of Jesus "crying out" for help; He is asking YHWH to provide Him (Jesus) with effective refuge through the Statutes/Decrees of YHWH (v. 145), the Testimonies/Statutes of YHWH (v. 146), and the word of YHWH (v. 147).

- In this v. 145, Jesus is committed to keeping the Statutes/Decrees of YHWH (there is no "and" in the Hebrew), but He doesn't want to do this alone without His Father (since that would be giving in to the agenda of the wicked party).

Question for you: Do you ever try to obey the Commands of God in your own strength? Is that relying on God to provide your righteousness?

146. "I call out to you; save me
      and I will keep your statutes." (NIV)

      Hebrew Literal: "I cried to you   save me
                      and I shall keep   your testimonies."

 Copyright © 2018, Richard L. Routh, All rights reserved.

Meditations and commentary:

- Here we have the "and." Jesus is crying out. I think this indicates an extreme sense of need. He is crying out for YHWH to save Him. But save Him from what? Save Him from capitulating to the wicked's agenda, namely: to keep the Testimonies/Statutes of YHWH on His own apart from the provision of YHWH.

Question for you: Did Jesus completely fulfill all the requirements for you to now be seen as perfectly right in God's sight? Is there anything left for you to fulfill?

147. "I rise before dawn and cry for help;
    I have put my hope in your word." (NIV)

Hebrew Literal: "I rise   before the dawn   and cry out
                    in   your word   I hoped."

Meditations and commentary:

- This crying out to YHWH for His help (intervention) has primacy in Jesus' priorities and schedule. It is so urgent that He cannot wait till the normal waking hour, but rises early before the sun is up. He knows YHWH will bring His provision through the Scriptures.

- Those of us who are now in Christ, who are habitual searchers of the word of God, know that searching the Scriptures without the help (interventional provision) of the Holy Spirit is futile. Anyone who is a serious seeker of solace and guidance from the word of God knows that two parts are necessary for success: one is the written word (the Scriptures), and the other is the Holy Spirit who gives us understanding of those Scriptures. It is this same two-part dynamic on which Jesus depends. To attempt to find truth in the word of YHWH without the additional illumination of YHWH is exactly what Jesus is trying to avoid, as that would be falling into the trap of the wicked (who are representing the proposition of Satan to find "good" by ourselves apart from God).

Question for you: Do you ever find yourself fervently crying out to God even though you already know He is going to provide what you ask? Why do you do that? Why did Jesus do that?

148. "My eyes stay open through the watches of the night,
     that I may meditate on your promises." (NIV)

Hebrew Literal: "<u>Anticipate</u>   <u>my eyes</u>   <u>the [night] watches</u>
                <u>that I might meditate</u>   <u>on your spoken word</u>."

Meditations and commentary:

- If you look at the Hebrew for this verse, it might occur to you (as it does to me) that one way to translate this verse into English might be: "I can hardly wait for each night watch to change because then I can wake up and meditate on Your word (as written in the Scriptures)."

  The darkness of the night was divided into three watch periods of about 4 hours each. A guard was posted to watch over a city or a camp through the night. This guard changed after each watch so that every night-guard could still get about 8 hours of sleep (and be up watching for the other four hours every night). This was a common night-time security measure in the ancient Roman and Hebrew world.

  There was commonly some noise and commotion associated with the changing of the guard at the end of each night watch. If you were a light (or alert) sleeper, you might be aroused at the changing of each watch. Perhaps what Jesus is saying here is that He very much looks forward to being awakened every four hours throughout the night so He can spend some time, even then, meditating on the word of YHWH. The point here is that for Jesus, there was an urgency and excitement and anticipation of being able to regularly (every four hours) meditate and pray through some portion of the word of YHWH. After spending the last three years of my life regularly praying through an octet of Psalm 119 every day, it would not surprise me to find that Jesus fervently prayed through an octet of Psalm 119 every four hours. If that were so, then in any 24 hour period of time, Jesus would have prayed through seven different octets of Psalm 119 (e.g.—6 a.m., 10 a.m., 2 p.m., 6 p.m., 10 p.m., 2 p.m., and 6 a.m.). If that were so, and I am only conjecturing about this, then this would shed some light on v. 164 which says, "Seven times a day I praise you for your righteous laws." I am not saying that Jesus only prayed an octet of this Psalm at those times, but it does occur to me that every four hours He would at least pray an octet of this Psalm.

  It is true that every single one of the 22 octets of Psalm 119 is a treatise on "praising YHWH for His righteous Laws" (v. 164).

Question for you: What are some things/activities in your life that function according to an established frequency (or cycle time)?

149. "Hear my voice in accordance with your love;
    preserve my life, YHWH, according to your laws." (NIV)

    Hebrew Literal: "<u>My voice</u>   <u>hear you</u>   <u>according to your covenant loyalty</u>
            <u>YHWH</u>   <u>according to your judgments</u>   <u>revive me</u>."

Meditations and commentary:

- The Hebrew root word "hesed," translated here in the NIV as "love," can also be translated as: "covenant loyalty," "covenant righteousness," "covenant commitment," "righteous promise," "lovingkindness," "mercy," "kindness," "favor." It is all of these concepts wrapped up into one word in Hebrew. Such a concept does not exist in English all in one place, but this Hebrew word means all these things all at once. Jesus is appealing to this covenant commitment that YHWH has promised to lovingly keep as a righteous obligation discharged with great kindness, to hear His (Jesus') voice (His cry or appeal) to revive Him (preserve His life) as prescribed and promised in YHWH's Laws and Judgments. That is a mouthful. It took me forty-two words to say in English what it takes just six words to say in the Hebrew! But my forty-two English words are saying just exactly what those six Hebrew words are saying.

- Jesus is asking to be revived. Why? Because He has been oppressed and emotionally beaten down to the point of near paralysis. Jesus sees His solution as a two-part solution. Part 1: His revival must be done in conformance with the promises and judgments of the Law of YHWH; and Part 2: The administration of this solution must be done personally by YHWH.

Question for you: Do you ever get delivered from trouble apart from God doing it as prescribed in His word?

150. "Those who devise wicked schemes are near,
   but they are far from your law." (NIV)

   Hebrew Literal: "<u>They draw near</u>   <u>who follow after</u>   <u>harm</u>
                      <u>from your law</u>   <u>they are far</u>."

AND

151. "Yet you are near, YHWH,
   and all your commands are true." (NIV)

   Hebrew Literal: "<u>[Are] near</u>   <u>you</u>   <u>YHWH</u>
                      <u>and all</u>   <u>your commands [are]</u>   <u>truth</u>."

Meditations and commentary:

- "They draw near" is a single word idiom in the Hebrew that conveys the notion of someone wanting to move more intimately into the social orbit of your relationship networks. Their intent, among other things, would be to have greater influence over you by trading on your natural affinity for friendship. I am convinced that because Jesus had such a great love for those around Him, that His natural (Godly) affinity for friendship was much stronger than it is for the rest of us. This means the pressure He felt to want to be able to conform to the agenda of these people was a very strong and compelling pressure. But at the same time, Jesus clearly understood that if He allowed them to have this influence that was natural to friendship, it would bring Him to harm because their agenda did not align with the Law of YHWH. So, their friendship was poison to Him, even though He had a strong desire to be friends with them. This incessant internal conflict begs the question: How is Jesus to have this need for deep friendship to be met in His life? The answer is in verse 151. YHWH Himself will be the "near" (close) friend that meets Jesus' need for friendship, and YHWH's friendship will not result in harm to Jesus because YHWH's friendship will be in complete alignment with His Commands which are always true—implication: always pure, wholesome, healthy, and constructive. This entire theme is re-echoed in First Corinthians 15:33.

  Question for you: Would you rather have the friendship of God, or the friendship of some other person? (This is not asking which you should prefer; it is asking which you actually do prefer.)

152. "Long ago I learned from your statutes
        that you established them to last forever." (NIV)

Hebrew Literal: "<u>Long ago</u> <u>I have known</u> <u>from your testimonies</u>
                  <u>that them</u> <u>forever</u> <u>you have founded</u>."

Meditations and commentary:

- When everything in your life seems to be fickle, unstable or futile; when it seems you can't really count on anything to be what it is supposed to be; when you find yourself betrayed by those you thought you could count on, then you are in the same spot that Jesus was in—indeed, He lived continually in that spot! What do you do when everything and everyone around you is unreliable, faulty, and imperfect? When you become aware that everyplace in the world you try to stand is unsteady, as if you were in a never-ending earthquake? You become desperate to find something solid and steady that you could hold onto, something you know that you can count on. In this verse, Jesus is saying that what is steady, reliable and always trustworthy are the Statutes/Testimonies of YHWH. The writings of Moses and the prophets, the Testimonies of YHWH that comprise those writings, were (and are) so solid and trustworthy that they remain something that can <u>always</u> be counted on. These are Jesus' anchor in a very tumultuous storm. This is the very solid hope to which Jesus clings. He knows they will never move because He has that guarantee from the eternal unchanging YHWH, who controls all things for all time, that they will never move. And now, Jesus Himself is that solid rock for us!

Question for you: What is it about having Jesus be your best friend that makes that be an undesirable proposition for you?

ר **Resh (200)** – Theme: I find life, hope, and deliverance in Your Law because Your tender mercies are contained in Your Judgments.

153. "Look upon my suffering and deliver me,
       for I have not forgotten your law." (NIV)

       Hebrew Literal: "<u>Consider</u>   <u>my affliction</u>   <u>and deliver me</u>
                        <u>for</u>   <u>your law</u>   <u>not</u>   <u>do do I forget</u>."

Meditations and commentary:

- Have you noticed how many verses in this psalm refer to suffering/affliction? This will hopefully help the reader to see that Isaiah 53:3 was an extreme understatement. It was also a description of Jesus' entire life, not just His crucifixion.

    He was despised and rejected by men,
    a man of sorrows, and familiar with suffering.
    Like one from whom men hide their faces
    He was despised, and we esteemed Him not. (Isaiah 53:3, NIV)

    So, again, the three main points we should never forget are:
    - Jesus' suffering was severe and relentless.
    - In the midst of His suffering He never lost His commitment to, or His focus on, the Law of YHWH.
    - He always looked only to YHWH to deliver Him through that Law and thereby provide relief from His affliction. (He never resorted to His own best efforts to get Himself out of the box.)

- **Question for you:** Jesus said, "Blessed are those who mourn, for they shall be comforted." If you were to ask Jesus how He received His suffering, affliction, and mourning, do you think He would say, "I'm glad for it all because then I get to experience the deliverance and comfort of YHWH"?

154. "Defend my cause and redeem me;

preserve my life according to your promise." (NIV)

Hebrew Literal: "<u>Plead</u>   <u>my cause</u>   <u>and deliver me</u>
<u>according to your spoken word</u>   <u>revive me</u>."

Meditations and commentary:

- In these two verses (vv. 153, 154) it appears that Jesus is highlighting the role differentiation between Himself and His Father as these pertain to Jesus' deliverance from His afflictions.

- The role of Jesus in v. 153 is to actively NOT FORGET the Law of YHWH, because in that Law does He find His deliverance. The role of His Father is to provide the deliverance as promised in these Laws.

- The use (and emphasis) of the Hebrew word "plead" gives the sense that Jesus is being tried in some sort of cosmic court. And indeed He is. By His incarnate life He has demonstrated total trust in the written word of YHWH, thereby establishing the case for the refutation of Satan's proposition, and the reasonableness for God's proposition. He is doing that in the cosmic court of all sentient beings across all of creation across all of time. In this court, Jesus is asking YHWH to be His lawyer and plead Jesus' case to uphold the reasonableness of the original intent of YHWH's spoken word.

Question for you: In the original Hebrew, Jesus often refers to the word of YHWH as the "spoken word" of YHWH. What percent of the time would you guess that "spoken word" came to Jesus in the form of the written word in the Old Testament Scriptures?

155. "Salvation is far from the wicked,
   for they do not seek out your decrees." (NIV)

Hebrew Literal: "<u>Far</u>   <u>from the wicked</u>   <u>[is] salvation</u>
<u>for</u>   <u>your statutes</u>   <u>not</u>   <u>do do they seek</u>."

Meditations and commentary:

- In contrast (to vv. 153 & 154), in this verse, Jesus is giving testimony and asking YHWH to plead the point in this cosmic court: that the prospects are hopeless for those who do not seek the Statutes of YHWH.

- It is very important that we do not lose sight of the truth that we do not naturally seek the Statutes of YHWH. But we who are in Christ can rely on the fact that Jesus <u>has</u> properly sought to keep the Statutes of YHWH, and that He did so in our place and to our credit.

Question for you: If someone gave you a lifetime membership in a very exclusive club in which the members were provided (free) all sorts of exciting wholesome activities and delicious healthy foods, would you use that membership often? Do you see that Jesus has purchased for you that sort of membership in the club of those who are allowed to live according to the Laws of YHWH without fear of any type of condemnation or personal criticism?

156. "Your compassion is great, YHWH,
    preserve my life according to your laws." (NIV)

Hebrew Literal: "<u>Your tender mercies [are]</u>   <u>great</u>   <u>YHWH</u>
                  <u>according to your judgments</u>   <u>revive me</u>."

Meditations and commentary:

- Do we think of the Judgments (see the Hebrew Literal) of God to be tender and merciful and efficacious for our deliverance and the preservation of our life? Jesus did. The Judgments of YHWH were powerful and desirable allies to which Jesus enthusiastically gravitated. We, on the other hand, have a strong natural tendency to run from them.

    And again (I continue to repeat this because it is at the core of what Jesus' passion for His mission was all about), the reason we have a natural tendency to run from the Judgments of YHWH is because it is our fallen nature to want ourselves to be the source of deciding what "good" looks like; our (fallen) nature rejects the proposition that we should desire, seek, and adhere to the Statutes/Judgments of YHWH. We are only willing to do so when the Statutes of YHWH happen to appear to line up with what we think is reasonable. The problem here, of course, is that we take upon ourselves to pass judgment on, and defend the reasonableness of, God's Decrees. So, we are willing to conform to the Laws of God as long as we get to be god.

- The real question here is whether or not our trust in the goodness of God is greater than our desire and ability to be the one to decide what "good" looks like. For Jesus, His trust in the goodness of YHWH was greater; indeed, it was the ONLY factor in the process of deciding what He would do.

Question for you: Do you see the judgments of God as tender mercies? Did Jesus see them that way? (See the Hebrew Literal for v. 156.)

157. "Many are the foes who persecute me,
     but I have not turned from your statutes." (NIV)

Hebrew Literal: "Many [are]   my persecutors   and my enemies
               [yet] from your testimonies   not   do I turn."

Meditations and commentary:

- It is clear from the entire context of Psalm 119 that Jesus is being persecuted because He consistently, without fail, follows the Statutes/Testimonies of YHWH. It is also clear from the entire context of Psalm 119 (and the rest of the Scriptures) that Jesus is faithfully adhering to the Statutes/Testimonies of YHWH in order to lay the foundation to provide for the rescue and deliverance of His persecutors and enemies (Romans 5:8-10).

- I do not see the verses of this octet so much as a complaint against those who set themselves up as the enemies of God (as Adam and Eve did), as it is a recognition and acceptance by Christ of His role to deliver us. This deliverance was done by His obedience, on our behalf. His obedience, in our place, is what delivers us from the inevitable destruction (the just wrath of the Holy God) of all of us who travel this path of rebellion. We oppose and fight all that Christ believes and stands for, and in return, He dies for us and thereby rescues us from the awful consequences of that willful opposition.

  If anyone could even remotely entertain the thought that they have not been consistently and vehemently opposed to the obedience of Christ, then that person has not been paying one wit of attention to anything happening throughout this Psalm (or anywhere else in Scripture, for that matter). And if anyone does not understand that Jesus saw it as His mission to provide them with full righteousness before God as He sits eternally on His Holy throne, then that person also has not been paying one wit of attention to anything that has

Behold the Christ   Copyright © 2018, Richard L. Routh, All rights reserved.

happened in the previous 156 verses.

Question for you: Where do you get your righteousness from? <u>All</u> of it?

158. "I look on the faithless with loathing,
    for they do not obey your word." (NIV)

Hebrew Literal: "<u>I beheld</u>   <u>the transgressors</u>   <u>and was grieved</u>
        <u>because</u>   <u>your spoken word</u>   <u>not</u>   <u>do have they kept</u>."

Meditations and commentary:

- Continuing on from the commentary for the previous verse (v. 157): Yes! Jesus is grieved (see the Hebrew) by our sin and that grief, filtered through His love for us, has moved Him to perform righteousness for us and then die in our place so that we might have that exchange (Second Corinthians 5:21) available to us. Our sin grieved Jesus, so He lived and died to buy us back with His life/blood. That is the measure of Christ's love for you. If we don't own up to our sin, which is our desire to figure out what is good apart from trusting God to tell us what is good, then we can never avail ourselves of Christ's deliverance for us.

Question for you: What do you conclude when Scripture tells us one thing and modern science (or even our own observations) tell us the exact opposite? Which source do you trust to have the correct answer?

159. "See how I love your precepts;
    preserve my life, YHWH, according to your love." (NIV)

Hebrew Literal: "<u>Consider</u>   <u>how</u>   <u>your precepts</u>   <u>I love</u>
        <u>YHWH</u>   <u>according to your covenant loyalty</u>   <u>revive me</u>."

Meditations and commentary:

- Again, Jesus saw it as His role to fully trust, and therefore obey, the precepts of YHWH; and He saw it as the Father's promised role to keep Him (Jesus) full of life, both before and after His crucifixion.

Question for you: Do you understand that in order for the Statutes of YHWH to be efficacious, they require the continual personal intervention of YHWH?

160. "All your words are true;
    all your righteous laws are eternal." (NIV)

    Hebrew Literal: "[From] the beginning   your word   [is] true
                      forever   every one   of your judgments   righteous."

    Meditations and commentary:

    - Here are some thoughts I have regarding the place of the Laws of YHWH in the new Earth (Revelation 21). The Laws/Judgments of YHWH have always been, always are, and always will be, true. This fact was the constant anchor of Jesus' hope. It is what brought Him (and I think still brings Him) continual joy.

        It is also why the New Earth will be a place without sorrow or pain. This (the truth and righteousness of the Judgments of YHWH) is the power behind how Jesus will make all things new (Revelation 21:5). It will not be because of our obedience, but because His righteousness has first provided us with full righteousness—and one of the glorious consequences of this new righteousness is that all the obstacles that kept us from walking in the righteous paths of YHWH's Laws will have been removed!

        Jesus will always be the only true Law Keeper, but now we can dance in the Law with Him without being concerned about getting a dance step wrong (Romans 8:1).

    - This verse (as well as all of Psalm 119) helps us to understand just a part of the impetus behind Jesus' saying in Matthew 5:19: "Therefore anyone who breaks one of the least of these commandments and teaches others to do the same will be called least in the kingdom of heaven, but whoever practices and teaches these commands will be called great in the kingdom of heaven."

    Question for you: Is the Law of God your friend?

ש **Shin (300)** – Theme: Great peace have they who love Your Law, and nothing can make them stumble!

161. "Rulers persecute me without cause,
    but my heart trembles at your word." (NIV)

    Hebrew Literal: "<u>Princes</u> <u>have persecuted me</u> <u>outside a cause</u>
                    <u>of</u> <u>your word</u> <u>stands in awe</u> <u>my heart</u>."

    Meditations and commentary:

    - Looking at all eight verses of this octet as a single whole, it appears to emphasize the realization that the heart is what drives the actions. Our heart is what determines our actions. And in Jesus' case, His <u>heart trembles</u> at YHWH's word (v. 161), <u>rejoices</u> in YHWH's word (v. 162), <u>loves</u> YHWH's Law (v. 163), <u>praises</u> for YHWH's Laws (v. 164), <u>love</u> for YHWH's Law brings peace (v. 165), <u>hope</u> (v. 166), and <u>love</u> of YHWH's Testimonies (v. 167). The results of His heart attitude(s) is(are): blamelessness (v. 161), great riches for His soul (v. 162), avoidance of falsehood (v. 163), praising YHWH (v. 164), peace and avoiding evil (v. 165), obeying the Commands of YHWH (v. 166), keeping the Statutes/Testimonies of YHWH (v. 167), and keeping YHWH's Precepts and Testimonies (v. 168). For Jesus, loving YHWH's Laws and keeping YHWH's Laws are inseparable things. You can't have one without the other.

    - Jesus' adherence to the word of YHWH was so perfectly complete, that even rulers who wanted to bring accusations of wrongdoing against Him could not find any legitimate ways of doing so. They were forced to only be able to make false accusations.

    - I praise You, Lord Jesus, because Your heart for, and obedience to, the Laws of YHWH were perfectly complete! And You have given that attitude and accomplishment to me and my brothers and sisters (2 Corinthians 5:21)!

    Question for you: If you are in Christ, do you recognize that God has written His Laws on your heart, and when you are walking by the Spirit, that affinity emerges?

162. "I rejoice in your promise

like one who finds great spoil." (NIV)

Hebrew Literal: "<u>Rejoice</u>   <u>I</u>   <u>at</u>   <u>your spoken word</u>
<u>as one who finds</u>   <u>spoil</u>   <u>great</u>."

Meditations and commentary:

- Jesus said in Matthew 6:19-21, "Do not store up for yourselves treasures on earth,... but store up for yourselves treasures in heaven. ...For where your treasure is, there your heart will be also." These verses in Matthew are not only a description of Jesus' attitudes toward the spoken words of YHWH, but they are also His advocacy for us to have this same attitude toward the spoken words of YHWH (as they are recorded in the Scriptures). This was prophesied in Jeremiah 31:33 and confirmed later in Hebrews 8:10, that God would write His Law on our hearts.

  What did Jesus value? (Note: This is just another way of asking the question, "What is it that has real value?") Jesus answers this in John 17:3 where He defines "eternal life" as experientially knowing God (longevity is just an almost inconsequential byproduct of this). <u>Real</u> value (<u>real</u> life) is experientially knowing God (Father and Son, according to John 17:3).

  For Jesus, experientially knowing YHWH was the only thing that mattered. It was <u>much</u> <u>much</u> <u>much</u> more important and valuable than winning the lottery, inheriting a billion dollars from a recently deceased relative, or any other means by which one might gain great earthly wealth. (Because, after all, the great earthly wealth will only decay, be destroyed by bugs, or be stolen; whereas knowing God will never be taken away from us and will return dividends to us in uncountable ways forever.)

  So, how did Jesus go about increasing His experiential knowledge of YHWH? By realizing that YHWH has revealed Himself through His spoken word, and that when Jesus kept and obeyed and followed those Laws, Precepts, Commands, and Testimonies of YHWH, He was experiencing the very heart and mind of YHWH. And according to John 17:4, when Jesus kept the Laws of YHWH, He was revealing YHWH to us. All of this has infinite eternal value (wealth) and that is why it was of so much more value to Jesus than "great spoil."

Question for you: What do you value more than deepening your relationship with God? (You can tell by whatever gives you greater delight than deepening your relationship with God.)

163. "I hate and abhor falsehood
     but I love your law." (NIV)

Hebrew Literal: "Lying   I hate   and abhor
                 [but] your law   do I love."

Meditations and commentary:

- Jesus Himself said that He was the truth (Greek: "aletheia"—means truth or revealed truth). Lies cannot exist in the presence of the truth any more than darkness can exist in the presence of light. The Law of YHWH is pure truth and contains no lies. Therefore, the Law of YHWH adheres so closely to the heart of Jesus that it is inseparable from, even indistinguishable from, Jesus.

  Question for you: What in your life is not aligned with the word and will of God? (You can tell by what you are willing to lie about, or at least prefer to remain hidden.)

164. "Seven times a day I praise you
     for your righteous laws." (NIV)

Hebrew Literal: "Seven times   a day   do I praise you
                 because of   your judgments   righteous."

Meditations and commentary:

- If you do something every four hours, then according to the way ancient Hebrews would count that, you would be doing it seven times a day.

- This is not the only thing about Jesus that had a continually cyclical periodic function. His heart beat every second or so, as does yours. His lungs breathed in and out about fifteen times every minute, as do yours. Many of your bodily organs and systems have a regular periodic, cyclical function. Jesus is saying here that this regular periodic, cyclical functioning applied also to His praising YHWH for His righteous Laws, and that the periodic cycle time for this activity, which was as regular for Jesus as His heart beating and His lungs breathing, was four hours. As I have already stated elsewhere in this commentary, it is my personal conjecture that every four hours Jesus prayed an octet of this psalm. This was the normal way that He kept spiritually breathing, just as He had a normal way that He kept physically breathing.

Question for you: Does this suggest anything to you?

165. "Great peace have they who love your law,
    and nothing can make them stumble." (NIV)

Hebrew Literal: "<u>Peace</u>   <u>great</u>   <u>have they who love</u>   <u>your law</u>
    <u>and nothing</u>   <u>to</u>   <u>stumbling [lead them]</u>."

Meditations and commentary:

- Satan is the one who whispers continuously in our ear, "Do your best! You can do this! Just work at it—you'll figure it out!" After all, that is exactly what he said to Eve in the Garden. Of course, the problem with that advice is that we now have six thousand years' worth of human history that, if it illustrates anything, it illustrates that when we "do our best," we make a shambles of it all.

- So, some people are tempted to ask, "What do you mean?!? Do you mean God will judge me for trying my best to do right?" Absolutely! And if you don't understand why the wrath of God is justly aimed at those who "do their best to be good," then you don't understand what was wrong with Satan's proposition to Eve, you don't understand that righteousness can only come to us when it is provided by God through Jesus Christ (given to us, earned by Christ, and not earned at all by us), and you don't understand your complete lack of ability to be righteous (and you don't understand the Gospel). One thing we should learn from Genesis 3 is that "doing our best to be good" is the essence of sin. Even if your heart were completely pure (which it is not), it would still be impossible for you to be righteous. We were not created with the capability or potential to be righteous on our own. It was always God's plan to provide that for us; it was always God's only plan to be the One who provides us with righteousness. This thought is consistent with the theme of Genesis 1-2, and it is highlighted by the counter-theme of Genesis 3:1-7.

    It would make even less sense to tell us to do our best to be righteous than it would to tell a fish to run a marathon on land in less than three hours. First of all, a fish cannot live on land for three hours; it would suffocate. Second, a fish does not have the right anatomy to be able to run a hundred feet, let alone twenty-six miles. Third, a fish cannot understand English, so it would never be able to understand the goal you would require of it, since there is nothing in its entire experience of existence that would even remotely be able to give that fish a rudimentary concept of running, breathing air, proper training and diet for a marathon, etc. Fourth, even if a fish could get a vision for what it means to run a marathon, it would be mentally incapable of the planning and execution necessary to actually run the marathon. All these, and a lot more, are metaphors of the same obstacles that face us when we attempt to be righteous by our own efforts.

From God's perspective, which is the only perspective that defines reality, it is a ludicrous proposition for us to attempt to be righteous. It is a ludicrous proposition for Satan to attempt to do the right thing and make good decisions on his own, but Satan never understood or accepted this. He tries to get us to believe in what he believes in, but it is futile for him and it is futile for us. Only God can know what good looks like in every situation, and He is willing to tell us and then lead us by the hand through it, if we will be completely dependent on Him to do so. And there is the rub! We are not always willing to be completely dependent on God's Law and God's leading. The good news (the Gospel) is that Jesus was always desirous of being, and committed to being, completely dependent on YHWH's Law and YHWH's leading. That is how He attained full righteousness; and then when He had fulfilled all the requirements for complete righteousness for us, He died in our place, exchanging with us His righteousness for our sin. In this way, God has provided us with righteousness. Of course, if we refuse to accept this gift by saying, "No, I don't need you to provide me with righteousness; I can do this by myself; after all, if I try my best, surely that will be good enough!" Then we are rejecting God in exactly the same way that Adam and Eve rejected God in His role of defining good for us.

- The finite cannot properly navigate the corridors of infinity, but the Infinite can hold the hand of the finite and properly lead him through those corridors. That is the only way to safely navigate those corridors. That is the only way to be at peace about the journey.

- Our peace now comes from accepting that Jesus was the One who properly trusted YHWH and His guidance (His Law) and who properly allowed YHWH to lead Him through these corridors. He did that for us, on our behalf, in our place.

Question for you: Do you want more peace in your life? How did Jesus get peace in His life? (See v.165)

166. "I wait for your salvation, YHWH,

and I follow your commands." (NIV)

Hebrew Literal: "<u>I have hoped</u>   <u>for your salvation</u>   <u>YHWH</u>
<u>and your commands</u>   <u>I do</u>."

Meditations and commentary:

- Godly "Hope" (Christian "Hope") is NOT the same thing as "wishing." It is certainly not wishing hard or wishing with all your might. Godly hope does not depend on something that comes from within us. Godly hope is when we <u>wait</u> for what God Himself has already guaranteed will happen as He told us in His word.

  Godly hope is when we wait, expecting that God did not lie when He told us something would happen. There is NO perceived uncertainty in the hope God gives us. YHWH sees all of the future as though it were already accomplished history. If you want to look at it like this, it would certainly be accurate: YHWH comes back in time from all the way to the end of an everlasting future history and tells us what is going to happen. From His perspective, our future has already happened.

  When God tells us something is going to happen, since it is impossible for God to lie (Hebrews 6:18), and since there is nothing iffy, uncertain, or unpredictable about what He is telling us will happen, then God is stating a fact, not expressing a wish, about something that has already happened in our future.

  So, the NIV has it right here when it translates the Hebrew word for "hope" as "wait." Jesus is waiting for a salvation He knows is coming. He knows it is certain because that is what YHWH has said will happen.

  A corollary to all this is that since YHWH's statements about what is true are so unflinchingly rock solid, and since part of what YHWH has stated to be good are His Commands, then it makes all the sense in the world (and in eternity) to Jesus that the Commands of YHWH should be obeyed, so He does. For Jesus, it would be irrational to take any other position.

- Another corollary to this is that it is irrational when WE do not follow the Commands of God. Perhaps it would be helpful to realize that the next time you consider taking an action that goes against one of the Commands of God is to see that action as insane. Do you really want to be a psychotic person? Because taking that action which is opposed to a Command of God reveals a very broken psyche ("psyche" is the Greek word for "soul").

- Being consistent with the truth is rational. Being inconsistent with the truth does not make sense. Jesus was always consistent with the truth as revealed through the Commands of YHWH.

Question for you: Have you ever before realized that acting in opposition to the Statutes of YHWH is psychotic? That it is a form of insanity?

167. "I obey your statutes,
    for I love them greatly." (NIV)

Hebrew Literal: "<u>Has kept</u>   <u>my soul</u>   <u>your testimonies</u>
            <u>and I love them</u>   <u>exceedingly</u>."

Meditations and commentary:

- (See the Hebrew Literal for this verse.)

- The needs of our body are met with physical things. The needs of our body are met by such physical things as food, water, oxygen, clothes, good health, etc. The needs of our soul are such things as Purpose, Joy, Freedom, Hope, Esteem, and a sense of Belonging. These "soul needs" can be met with either physical things (but as we have said, these physical soul satisfiers are illusory and temporary), or we can get our soul needs met with the Very Person of God as He is revealed to us His Statutes/Testimonies, which is not really distinguishable from the way He is revealed to us through the life and Person of Jesus Christ.

- Jesus got His soul's needs met through the Statutes/Testimonies of YHWH and this resulted in Him having an exceeding and increasing love for those Statutes that bring this deep and lasting satisfaction to His soul.

Question for you: Did you realize that getting your soul's needs met by things in this world is a characteristic of your fallen nature; versus getting your soul's needs met by the very Person of God is characteristic of your new nature in Christ?

Also, have you realized that when you are getting your soul's needs met by seeking the face of God that you are walking by the Spirit; versus when you are getting your soul's needs met by things that you do in this physical world, that you are walking by the flesh?

168. "I obey your precepts and your statutes,
    for all my ways are known to you." (NIV)

Hebrew Literal: "<u>I have kept</u>   <u>your precepts</u>   <u>and your testimonies</u>
              <u>for</u>   <u>all</u>   <u>my ways</u>   <u>are before you</u>."

Meditations and commentary:

- A lot of people may see this verse as a statement of only one-way accountability. Specifically, Jesus is accountable to His Father to ensure that He (Jesus) keeps His Father's precepts and Statutes/Testimonies. And indeed it is that.

- But I see this verse as also a celebration and praise to the Father that recognizes a two-way accountability. Jesus knows the Father has seen ahead and knows all the things Jesus will need. All of this foreknowledge went into the crafting (this is a metaphor) of all the Precepts and Statutes/Testimonies by YHWH to ensure that Jesus would have all His needs met by keeping those Precepts and Statutes/Testimonies. In this sense, the Precepts and Statutes of YHWH were a roadmap, custom tailored to Jesus' specific needs, that embodied the full love and faithfulness and provision of the Father for His Son. (This psalm is an example of that type of provision.)

- It is helpful for us to realize that the Precepts and Testimonies of YHWH provide that same benefit (the meeting of our needs) for us.

Question for you: According to this Psalm 119, what could you do to take greater advantage of the provisions and benefits God has for you? (Hint: It does not involve trying harder to do anything.)

 Copyright © 2018, Richard L. Routh, All rights reserved.

ת **Taw (400)** – Theme: Deliver Me, when I start to get disoriented, by increasing my understanding of Your Law so I can proclaim the righteousness of Your Commands.

169. "May my cry come before you, YHWH,
       give me understanding according to your word." (NIV)

   Hebrew Literal: "<u>Let come near</u>   <u>my cry</u>   <u>before you</u>   <u>YHWH</u>
                   <u>according to your word</u>   <u>give me understanding</u>."

   Meditations and commentary:

   - We humans are in constant need of emphasizing a proper focus. Our brains are constantly being bombarded with a myriad of diverse sensory inputs that would distract us from this focus unless we are vigilant in keeping it. Jesus knew His focus should remain on making sure that all His understanding found its source in the word of YHWH, and here He is crying and pleading for YHWH to make sure that happens. This verse not only emphasizes Jesus' heart to ensure His understanding remains aligned with, and always formed by, the word of YHWH, but this verse also emphasizes Jesus' commitment to not attempt to do this by Himself, but to always rely on the provision of YHWH to ensure it happens.

   - I'm not sure this is intended to be a summary of this major theme that recurs throughout Psalm 119, but it does function as such.

   Question for you: Is it possible for a person to get true understanding of the word of God without having God reveal its truth to them?

170. "May my supplication come before you;
       deliver me according to your promise." (NIV)

   Hebrew Literal: "<u>Let come</u>   <u>my supplication</u>   <u>before you</u>
                   <u>according to your spoken word</u>   <u>deliver me</u>."

Meditations and commentary:

- Jesus' deliverance is not in doubt in this verse. Jesus is God, and God cannot be extinguished.

- Jesus is not just asking to be delivered. He is asking that when His deliverance comes, that it comes in such a way so that it conforms to the spoken word of YHWH. When Jesus was responding to Satan's first temptation in the wilderness (Matthew 4:1-4), He was not rejecting bread. Jesus knew He would not be left by His Father to die of starvation. Jesus was rejecting bread unless it came to Him in accordance with the spoken word of YHWH (the written Scriptures). Jesus was not willing to have His needs met in any way that did not completely conform to that which was prescribed in the word of YHWH.

- It was not acceptable to Jesus that He be delivered in any way other than that which was in accordance to the spoken word of YHWH. (This is why He rejected Satan's proposal to provide for His own needs from His own strength with His own plan, but instead, He countered Satan by reasserting His reliance on the fact that, "Man shall not live on bread alone, but on every word that comes from the mouth of God.") That is what Jesus is praying for in this verse. As we have seen, a primary theme of Psalm 119 is that ultimately Jesus was praying here for our deliverance, because our deliverance was contingent on Jesus being delivered in accordance with the Scriptures.

- Based on the full context of Psalm 119, I think v. 170 could be accurately translated into English in the following way:

  "My plea is that You, YHWH, not allow my deliverance to come in any way other than that which conforms to Your spoken word (in the Scriptures)."

Question for you: What is the ultimate outcome when you are apparently delivered from trouble, but it is not in accordance with the word of God?

171. "May my lips overflow with praise,
    for you teach me your decrees." (NIV)

Hebrew Literal: "Shall overflow   my lips   with praise
                when   you have taught me   your statutes."

Meditations and commentary:

- It is the Father's role to provide for us by presenting to us in His word what His will is for us, and what the means are to be for implementing that will in our lives. Furthermore, it is the Father's role to lead us through how all that comes together to be the full and complete satisfaction of our needs. It is our role to accept only that means for the satisfaction of our needs and to be so filled with awe and gratitude for how He does it that our hearts overflow with praise for His goodness and His provision. It is this dual-role dynamic that Jesus was praising His Father for here in this verse (v. 171).

Question for you: In your own words, what is the "dual-role dynamic" described in the above paragraph?

172. "May my tongue sing of your word,
    for all your commands are righteous." (NIV)

Hebrew Literal: "<u>Shall speak</u>   <u>my tongue</u>   <u>of your spoken word</u>
          <u>for</u>   <u>all</u>   <u>your commands</u>   <u>[are] righteous</u>."

Meditations and commentary:

- It is the Father's will to provide for us through His word [which ultimately means His Word—the λόγος (logos) of God, i.e., Christ (John 1)]. That fact is proclaimed by Jesus in Matthew 4:4 when Jesus says, "It is written...but on every word that comes from the mouth of God." This proclamation of Jesus in Matthew 4:4 was the rule by which Jesus lived His life. This proclamation in Matthew 4:4 is also one of the many places in which Jesus fulfills the claim made in this v. 172.

Question for you: Without using the words "righteousness" or "right," in your own words describe what it means when this verse (v. 172) says, "all your commands are righteous."

173. "May your hand be ready to help me,
    for I have chosen your precepts." (NIV)

Hebrew Literal: "<u>Let</u>   <u>your hand</u>   <u>help me</u>
                <u>for</u>   <u>your precepts</u>   <u>I have chosen</u>."

Meditations and commentary:

- As we have said, life is an infinitely [this word is not an exaggeration] complex puzzle, because life proceeds from and reflects God, and God is an infinite being. We, on the other hand, at least in our physical being, are finite. In our hearts we may well yearn to have our life conform in every way to the Precepts of YHWH, as Jesus did so yearn. But our brains are finite. If we were to rely on our brains to figure out how to properly keep and follow the Precepts of YHWH, we would fail. On our best day it is still a ludicrous proposition to think that a finite mind could solve an infinitely complex puzzle. If we, on our best day, tried with all our strength, and mind, and heart, to follow the Precepts of YHWH, we could not do it by ourselves because it is impossible for a finite, incarnate being to comprehend the full mind and purposes of the infinite will of YHWH. Jesus knew that. The Precepts of YHWH are only a piece of the solution to life's puzzle for us. They (His Precepts) are a necessary and crucial part of that solution for us, but they are not sufficient. YHWH did not give us His Law and then expect us to keep it by our own strength. It has always been His intent to take us by the hand and lead us through that infinite puzzle of how to properly apply His Precepts in our lives. Jesus knew this and He relied on this truth in order to properly keep the Precepts of YHWH.

  Question for you: If you decide to follow the Precepts of God in some given situation, according to this verse, what else do you have to do to experience a successful outcome?

174. "I long for your salvation, YHWH,
       and your law is my delight." (NIV)

    Hebrew Literal: "<u>I have longed</u>   <u>for your salvation</u>   <u>YHWH</u>
                     <u>and your law</u>   <u>[is] my delight</u>."

Meditations and commentary:

- In the context of the previous verse (v. 173), "salvation" here refers to the proper keeping of the Precepts of YHWH. Here Jesus is testifying that He longs for and delights in the Law of YHWH. This is necessary context for v. 176, the last and final (concluding) thought of this longest prayer in all of Scripture.

Question for you: Whose salvation was a stake in this verse?

175. "Let me live that I may praise you,
    and may your laws sustain me." (NIV)

    Hebrew Literal: "<u>Let live</u>   <u>my soul</u>   <u>and it shall praise you</u>
                    <u>and let your judgments</u>   <u>help me</u>."

    Meditations and commentary:

    - Life comes from God. Jesus' incarnate life and soul was given to Him by YHWH. Jesus looks to YHWH to maintain His life (His soul), and in return, Jesus, from His soul, praises YHWH, and in return, the judgments of YHWH will be a help to Jesus. This symbiotic relationship in the God-head is from eternity.

    - If we view our obedience to God's word as our gift to God, then we are completely missing the point and we have perverted Divine provision. The truth is that when we properly obey God and His word, it is God's gift to us—not our gift to God. In the context of justice, God does not owe us anything when we obey His Commands; instead, we owe God for our obedience since our obedience is by His gracious and merciful provision. Without God completely doing it, there would be no obedience on our part.

    Question for you: Have you yet come to view the judgments of God as your faithful helpers?

176. "I have strayed like a lost sheep.
    Seek your servant,
    for I have not forgotten your commands." (NIV)

    Hebrew Literal: "<u>I have gone astray</u>   <u>as a sheep</u>   <u>lost</u>
                    <u>seek</u>   <u>your servant</u>
                    <u>for</u>   <u>your commands</u>   <u>not</u>   <u>do have I forgotten</u>."

    Meditations and commentary:

- If we are not careful, it could appear that this wording and meaning is similar to that expressed in Isaiah 53:6. But a careful reading of this verse will see that it stands in contrast to Isaiah 53:6. Isaiah 53:6 is predicated on the fact that we have turned our own way—that we have risen up in rebellion against God and His word (per Genesis 3:1-7). Jesus, on the other hand, by the testimony of this very verse (v. 176), has <u>NOT</u> forgotten (or turned away from) the Commands of YHWH. Jesus' heart and actions are consistently and faithfully to long for and delight in the Law of YHWH (see vv. 174 & 175). What Jesus is recognizing in this last verse of Psalm 119 is that even when our heart and intent is right, righteousness is provided by God. (See also Luke 2:52)

  In contrast, <u>our</u> heart and intent is <u>not</u> right (because of our fallen nature). Our righteousness can only be provided by YHWH, but because of our waywardness, YHWH provides us with righteousness by first having Jesus accomplish its full measure for us, and then laying on Him our iniquity and crushing Him as a substitution in our place, so He might exchange with us His righteousness for our sin (Second Corinthians 5:21),... if we accept the offer.

Question for you: How would you explain to a non-Christian what it means to "accept the offer," in words they would understand? This often means you cannot use "religious" words (such as "saved," "faith," "sin," etc.), because other people will often not understand or define these words as you do.

APPENDIX A: Musings of the Author on The Mission of the Christ

Jesus came to redeem us from the Fall. Overcoming and reversing the effects of all the sin and death that began when Eve consented to the temptation of Satan, was an essential part of the reason He came to earth. To reverse the effects of Satan's proposition, He had to demonstrate that it was a faulty proposition. Essentially, Jesus came to demonstrate that it was actually better to trust God completely and to rely completely on His provisions as revealed through His spoken word—as opposed to asserting our independence to decide for ourselves what is fair (First John 3:8). The way He demonstrated this is chronicled for us in detail in Psalm 119. In order to give proper context to what Jesus was trying to accomplish as it is testified to us through the verses in Psalm 119, we need to understand what the problem was. That problem is laid out for us in the first three chapters of Genesis. Let's take a look at this and let's start with the first eight verses of Chapter 3.

The Eve Temptation

Genesis 3:

> **1** Now the serpent was more crafty than any of the wild animals the LORD God had made. He said to the woman, "Did God really say, 'You must not eat from any tree in the garden'?"
> **2** The woman said to the serpent, "We may eat fruit from the trees in the garden,
> **3** but God did say, 'You must not eat fruit from the tree that is in the middle of the garden, and you must not touch it, or you will die.' "
> **4** "You will not certainly die," the serpent said to the woman.
> **5** "For God knows that when you eat from it your eyes will be opened, and you will be like God, knowing good and evil."
> **6** When the woman saw that the fruit of the tree was good for food and pleasing to the eye, and also desirable for gaining wisdom, she took some and ate it. She also gave some to her husband, who was with her, and he ate it.
> **7** Then the eyes of both of them were opened, and they realized they were naked; so they sewed fig leaves together and made coverings for themselves.
> **8** Then the man and his wife heard the sound of the LORD God as he was walking in the garden in the cool of the day, and they hid from the LORD God among the trees of the garden.

Satan's Proposition

Summary of Satan's proposition to Eve:

1. You will not die. (Implication: The physical part of your existence is more important (valid) than the spiritual part of your existence.)
2. Your eyes will be opened. (Implication: What **YOU** see is what counts. What **YOU** perceive to be true is more valid than what you might think God has said is true. Therefore, you should become reliant on what you observe and what you can infer from those observations.)
3. You will be like God, knowing good and evil. (Implication: It is not good for God to be in the place to dictate to you what is good and what is not. Instead of being dependent on God for all your perceptions and judgments, you will be better if you are the one to be able to judge for yourself what is important and what is not. It will be better for you if you are the one to decide what is good (fair) and what is evil (not fair). Don't you want to have the right to decide what is fair? Do you really want someone else, God in this case, to be able to dictate to you what it fair? Doesn't your opinion count? Yes, you are important enough for your opinion to count. Assert your independence! Show them that you count for something and that you are important!)

Satan was not thinking that he was speaking falsehood. Satan was proposing an "alternate truth." This alternate truth was, by his way of thinking, better than that which was "proposed" by God.

Satan convinced himself that in order to be justified in his thinking, he would have to convince all of the cosmic audience (all the hosts of sentient witnesses, angelic and human, through all of time) that His way of seeing reality was more valid than God's way of seeing reality. This is the essence of a lie. It is why people become increasingly convinced of the validity of their lies. This is what was happening to Satan. He had something to prove to all of sentient creation, and he wanted to prove it, and he wanted his proof to stand the test of time, and to be recognized as a better alternate truth than the one "proposed" by God. This is what he convinced a third of the angelic host to accept: that it was a superior truth to the one put forth by YHWH. This is what he was tempting Eve to accept.

His motivation for this was envy (self-worship). He was supposed to be the highest created being. Hadn't God said so? Now God was proposing to create inferior beings (inferior because they were physical and much more limited intellectually than he was), indwell them with His Holy Spirit (an intimacy and identity with God that was not available to Satan), and include them in a more intimate way in the God-head than was offered to Satan. (See John 17:21.)

In order to prove for all to see that mankind was inferior to Him, he would get them to accept being relegated to a predominantly physical existence and to then get them to try to make things work in that new set of circumstances. If they succeeded, they would fail (because they would be excluding the spiritual world in their success). If they failed, they would fail. The result of this failure would be that Satan will have proven his point that He is the only one worthy of being called the highest created being.

Satan hated God's plan. He hated that God was intending to bestow His immeasurable grace on inferior beings. To Satan, this was ridiculous. It was ludicrous. It was insane. And the proper thing to do was to demonstrate to all that it was a plan that was not logical and could not stand the test of time.

So, he went to Eve with the proposition outlined in Genesis 3:4-5 (along with the precursor to this proposition as presented in Genesis 3:1).

God's "Proposition"

The background as it is recorded for us in Genesis Chapters One and Two is essential to gaining a fuller understanding of what is going on in first eight verses of Chapter Three.

In Genesis Chapter One, we read of a loving and good God who created a gloriously beautiful and rich world and gave it to our first parents. No sin. No sorrow. No death. No disappointments. And perfect fellowship with God. God had provided all they needed and could want. In this first chapter, we see that God's intent and behavior toward people was one where He provided all we could need and enjoy—and He did it completely out His generosity and His will. These provisions were not based on anything we did, which is evidenced by the fact that all was accomplished for us before we were even created, so we could not possibly claim or even think that we had anything at all to do with these blessings. The magnitude of God's blessing was enormous. Essentially, He provided an entire universe for our benefit. This was an evidence that God was able and intended to provide for all our needs and enjoyments from His infinite (not just abundant, but infinite) resources. These resources proceeded from the very person of who God was, as evidenced by the fact that He spoke them into existence.

In Genesis Chapter Two, we read about God assigning roles to the man and the woman. These roles were not a burden. They were exciting and fulfilling. The picture we have of the way things were made to work is one where God provides everything that is good and good for us. Our job was NOT to provide these things, or to decide what was good. Our job was just to enjoy the goodness God provided for us. We also see in second half of Chapter Two that God was protecting Adam and Eve by telling them what was good and what was not good for them to do.

The Consequences of Accepting Satan's Proposition

When Adam and Eve accepted Satan's proposal, they essentially had accepted the challenge to "make a go of it" as judges of good and evil, independent of the provision and judgments of God. From now on, they would be the ones to decide what was fair. They were asserting it was their right to do so. But this was a right appropriated apart from the will and provision of God. It is VERY important to recognize that when Adam and Eve decided to accept Satan's proposition to make a go if it independent from God, they were also making a decision to not avail themselves of the infinite spiritual resources that proceed from the very personhood of God. They were consciously choosing to separate themselves from God. This was their death—a chosen separation from the person and infinite provisions of God. They were restricting the scope of what they were to value to those things they could perceive with their physical senses apart from the identity of God. It is VERY important to recognize that they were restricting the scope of the resources available to them to only those that already existed in the physical world. No longer would they have access to the infinite resources that would have otherwise been available to them because those infinite resources proceed from the very person of God.

So, here is an abbreviated list of the consequences of Eve accepting Satan's proposal. You will recognize these as aspects and constraints and values of "human nature," or otherwise known as our fallen, or carnal, nature. Scripture also refers to this as the "natural" man.

- A deep and abiding conviction that it is a right and good thing that I get to decide what is good and what is not good. I get to decide what is fair. If something does not seem fair to me, then I do not consider it a good thing.

- The decisions about what is good/fair and what is not, will be made exclusively with my physical faculties: I will only consider data that comes from observations I (or others I trust) can see or otherwise measure with instruments that measure only physical things. Something is "real" only when you can touch it, see it, smell it, taste it, or otherwise verify its physical existence with trusted instruments that measure physical things.

- "I believe it when I see it." Not only will I only believe, and trust, those things that I can see, but it is not a matter so much of what I see as it is a matter of what I perceive them to be. My subjective judgment is king.

- Something is real (worthy of consideration, and worthy of being valued) only if it exists and can be observed in the physical world. This means that I discount spiritual solutions because they are not as powerful in satisfying my needs as physical solutions.

- A preference to favor "practical" solutions over "principled" decisions. The practical solution is better at immediately alleviating the discomfort of the most significant momentary detractor.

- Because I am the one who determines what is good in the world around me, and because I have only limited physical resources available to accomplish that goodness, then it is dependent on me to make things better by engaging in wise exchanges of my time, energy and physical wealth to maximize those "good" outcomes. These wise "equitable exchanges" are the currency of my success in this world.

- I will seek to satisfy my soul's needs of such things as purpose, joy, freedom, hope, esteem and belonging through the physical side of my being. So, the satisfaction of my need for purpose will come from my achievements (those times when I "successfully" made wise exchanges of my time, energy and physical wealth to maximize good outcomes). My joy comes from when I make exchanges that result in increasing my physical pleasures and comforts, make me more desirable to others, or increase my status in the eyes of others. My freedom comes from when I make wise exchanges that maximize my ability to do what I choose to do and minimize constraints to the contrary. My hope comes from when my exchanges maximize the apparent future potential for favorable outcomes for me in the physical world. My esteem comes from when others commend me for the wise exchanges I make. My sense of belonging comes from when others want me because of my ability to help the group with wise exchanges I make.

- All of the above items in this list are problematic and ultimately unfulfilling and all lead to the death of my soul because of the following:
  - Because there are limited physical resources, then those things that maximize my good (outcomes that are favorable to me) will sometimes be at odds with what other people consider their good (outcomes that are favorable to them). This will unavoidably result in tensions, struggling with others over how resources are to be utilized, discounting the needs and value of others, hatred that comes from being threatened by others who will want to use resources that do not maximize my good outcomes, envy, murder, etc.
  - The value and utility of spiritual solutions that come from the identity and person of God will be minimized, because these solutions are not part of the physical resources available to me that allow me to affect the world around me (for my good).
  - I, and others, will continually make exchange decisions that favor the immediate relief of the most salient discomfort as perceived at the moment. This will have the effect of constantly trading away greater benefits in the future for lesser benefits in the here and now. In other words, the world will continue to degrade around me and it will always be that the current path we are on will eventually impoverish us all. In other words, we are trapped in hopelessness. For example, like it or not, the fact is we all will physically die and thereby be compelled to forfeit ALL our time, energy, and worldly wealth.
  - Because of the law of rising expectations (a characteristic I believe God created in all who are created in His image, and one that He intended from the beginning to continually satisfy until our first parents stopped Him from doing so), and because the resources available to us are limited, we will always end up falling short of satisfying our soul needs. Therefore, we will continually be disappointed because we cannot get what we need to be fulfilled.

I could go on and on about the consequences of the Fall, but all of human history chronicles those consequences for us: crime, murders, war, disease, injustices, death, etc. AND ALL THESE NEGATIVE CONSEQUENCES ARE THE RESULT OF NOT COMPLETELY RELYING ON THE GRACIOUS PROVISIONS OF A LOVING WISE GOD, BUT INSTEAD CHOOSING TO FIND SOLUTIONS WITHIN OURSELVES. Note: This strategy of Satan was evident in the temptation of Christ in the wilderness when Satan tried to convince Jesus to use His own power to alleviate his hunger needs, instead of waiting trustingly on the timing and provision of YHWH (Matthew 4:1-4).

The Activities of Psalm 119

This temptation as recorded in Matthew 4:1-4 is a reassertion of Satan's original proposition to Eve. If Satan can get Jesus to rely on Himself instead of on the provisions of YHWH as revealed in His word (which is a picture of His very person), then all will be lost for us. If Satan could have gotten Jesus to use His own divine powers to satisfy his legitimate and extreme hunger needs, then the proposition that Satan made to Eve would have still stood, and God's "proposition" to provide all our needs from His graciousness generosity would have continued to be repudiated. Jesus was the second/last Adam. And as such, Jesus, by choosing NOT to use His own divine powers to alleviate His suffering and satisfy His need, was effectively repudiating Satan's proposition—and the cosmic audience was taking note of that! This, then, is the motivation and mission of the incarnate Christ—to repudiate the proposition of Satan that we should be the ones to decide when and how to cause "good" to happen. Jesus was here, at least in part, to demonstrate to all (the cosmic audience) that it is a reasonable, even preferred, path through life to rely exclusively on the provisions of YHWH as revealed to us through His word. Chronicling and demonstrating what that looks like is what Psalm 119 is all about.

Appendix B: Author's Answers to the Questions

Some readers have expressed a desire to see how the author would answer the questions asked in this book. This appendix responds to that request.

57. **Question for you:** Can anyone other than Jesus keep a promise to always obey the word of YHWH?

    No. I certainly will not and cannot. This is something that Jesus has done for me, and only He could.

58. **Question for you:** In your own words, please explain the main point being made by Jesus in John 17:3.

    What matters, the only thing that really matters, is becoming increasingly intimate with God the Father and God the Son.

59. **Question for you:** When Jesus said, "I thought on my ways" (see the Hebrew Literal), what kind of things specifically do you think He was thinking about?

    Am I hearing everything I need to be hearing from the word of YHWH regarding what I am thinking, feeling, and doing at this moment? Am I understanding the word of YHWH deep enough to think and feel and act more wisely here?

60. **Question for you:** What is the "oxygen" of your life? What causes you to become more enthusiastically engaged in life?

    Seeing the glories of God the Father, God the Son, and God the Holy Spirit more clearly is my oxygen.

61. **Question for you:** When Jesus says here "the bands of the wicked have encircled me" (see the Hebrew Literal), if the word "bands" is not intended to be literal ropes, then metaphorically what else might these "bands" be?

The obstacles the wicked attempt to put in Jesus' way to try to trip Him up and make His life more difficult, and to attempt to constrain Him and limit His impact

62. **Question for you:** When you think about the Ten Commandments, are there any of those ten that make you think, "Wow! I sure am glad God has committed Himself to enforcing that one among humans!"?

All of them. They are all gifts and blessings to me to increase my joy and fullness of life.

63. **Question for you:** Here the N.I.V. translates the Hebrew word for "keep" to be the English word "follow." In most places in this psalm, the N.I.V. translates the Hebrew word "keep" to be the English word "obey." Is there a difference between "keeping" and "obeying"? If so, what do you think that difference might be?

"Keeping" is more "consistent seeking and valuing." It results in "obeying," but "keeping" is more about attitude and motivation, whereas "obeying" is more about behavior.

64. **Question for you:** Have you ever thought of the Laws of Physics and Mathematics as being corollaries of the Laws of Moses?

Yep. That's why I wrote this question.

65. **Question for you:** Would it be good for us to view the word of YHWH in this way? We who are in Christ do view the Word of YHWH (Jesus) in this way, but would it also be good for us to view the word of YHWH (the spoken words of YHWH that comprise the Scriptures) in this way, as Jesus did?

Yes. If Jesus loved it, then I will love it! But "it" is more than "it," because "it" (the Law) is a testimony of, and extension of, the character and person of God (YHWH). So one way to love God is to know Him through His word.

66. **Question for you:** How would your life be different if you trusted YHWH to be faithful to you in accordance with the promises (explicit and implicit) contained in His Commands?

More love, joy, peace, patience, kindness, gentleness, self-control (bad word choice), and faithfulness. Better judgment. <u>I would know (γνωσις) God better!</u>

67. **Question for you:** If God the Father loved Jesus, why would He let Jesus be afflicted?

Because Jesus is the prototype human. Affliction leads to greater wisdom, which leads to deeper gnosis of God, which is "real" life, which is the only thing of value.

68. **Question for you:** Can you list 5 good things we discover about the Person of God by studying His Decrees/Statutes?

1. *His mercy*
2. *His commitment to holiness and justice*
3. *What truth looks like*
4. *What He values as "good"*
5. *His wisdom and faithfulness*

69. **Question for you:** What is it about Jesus that makes the proud want to accuse Him?

His absolute unflinching commitment to not make any decision or take any action or speak any word that is not revealed to Him by YHWH from His word, because this commitment repudiates the potential legitimacy of our sin nature.

70. **Question for you:** How are being "proud" and not delighting in the Law of God connected? Does "not delighting" in God's Law cause one to be proud, or does being proud cause one to not delight in God's Law, or is it both?

Both, but the "not delighting" comes first. The second one (pride) reinforces the "not delighting."

71. **Question for you:** Is affliction necessary if we are to learn the Statutes of God? Why? How does affliction relate to growing in wisdom?

> *Evidently. Because it was necessary for Jesus. Does it help keep our body subordinate to our spirit? It certainly motivates us to look deeper into what God is saying to us.*

72. **Question for you:** Would you be willing to trade $100 million dollars in lottery winnings for a better understanding of the Law of God?

> *Not sure. Probably not. But God is working that trade for me. It is why I have never won the lottery. I do rejoice in His will and trust it more than my own.*

73. **Question for you:** What is the reason the incarnate Jesus gives in this verse for why YHWH should give Him understanding to learn His Commands?

> *It is YHWH's intent to give us understanding to learn His commands and He designed us specifically for that purpose.*

74. **Question for you:** We all need hope. Without it humans quickly die. Where did Jesus get hope from?

> *He got His hope from the trustworthiness of YHWH's word.*

75. **Question for you:** For you, what are some of the "ensuing benefits" that you get from Jesus' accomplishments?

> - *Peace with God; a life of no condemnation*
> - *Light in my life where otherwise there would be darkness*
> - *Solid hope in the promises of God in His word*
> - *Allowed to boldly approach the throne of God*

76. **Question for you:** Do you regularly go to the word of God for the comfort of your soul?

> *Yes. I have to. I can find comfort nowhere else.*

77. **Question for you:** Do you see the Law of God as a vehicle by which you are brought the tender mercies of God?

I do now. Before this book, I did not.

78. **Question for you:** What remedy is recommended by this verse for when you are falsely accused? How would that work in your life?

Meditating on the Precepts of YHWH. When I am falsely accused, read this psalm and be comforted by knowing that I am experiencing what Jesus experienced, both in the false accusation, and in the comfort from the mind and heart of YHWH.

79. **Question for you:** Has it ever occurred to you that the greatest treasure you could get out of this life is the depth of the knowledge and relationship you have with God The Father and His Son, Jesus? (See John 17:3)

Yes, but doesn't that depth come through affliction? If so, that makes me hesitant. Oh Lord, make me to not be hesitant to embrace affliction is that's what's required to know you better.

80. **Question for you:** If Jesus had ever chosen to figure out and implement, on His own, a solution to a problem He had instead of waiting for YHWH to reveal it to Him from His word, would He still have been qualified to save us?

I think not. So, how do I live so that nothing I do or think or say is "the best that I can do," but instead I wait on revelation from the Holy Spirit as He speaks through the word of God?

81. **Question for you:** Have you ever considered that maybe you are most useful in God's hands when you are in the midst of great failure in your life?

Yes. And that paradox would not be so powerful if it were not so puzzling.

82. **Question for you:** In His prayer to YHWH in verse 81, Jesus refers to Scripture as "your word," but in His prayer in this verse (v. 82), Jesus refers to Scripture as "your spoken word." Why do you think Jesus sometimes calls Scripture the "word" of YHWH, and other times He calls it the "spoken word" of YHWH?

I suspect, at least in part, this is a reference to Genesis 1 where God spoke the world into existence. Scripture is one manifestation of the spoken word of YHWH.

83. **Question for you:** Like Jesus, do you sometimes have to face the fact that your life is in the process of being destroyed? Like Jesus, when you face this realization, do you find comfort in the Statutes and Decrees of God as they appear in Scripture?

Yes, that is what growing old is all about. Absolutely do I find comfort in the Scriptures!

84. **Question for you:** In what ways do you persecute Jesus?

When I join the arrogant and think it is ludicrous for us who are in Christ to abandon the proposition of us trying our best to do good, then I am persecuting Christ and dragging His finished work through the mud.

85. **Question for you:** Which of the above listed arrogances seem most compelling for you?

Answered above (in the text of the commentary).

86. **Question for you:** When you are tempted, do you try to resist the temptation by trying really hard to avoid it, or do you search Scripture asking God to show you how He has already provided the way of escape? Which approach did Jesus use?

Sometimes, but not often enough.
The second approach.

87. **Question for you:** Do you think this was a frequent struggle for Jesus, that He was "almost wiped" from the earth? Would it surprise you to discover that He faced this more often than you do?

I suppose it was a constant daily struggle. No, that would not surprise me.

88. **Question for you:** Do you ever feel like God should bless your life because you have been obedient to Him? Do you understand that feelings (and expectations) like that are part of your fallen nature, and not ever the way Jesus thought?

Less and less as time goes by am I inclined to think God will bless me because I have earned His blessing; and more and more am I trusting in the goodness of God to bless me (because God is good; not because I am good).

89. **Question for you:** Can you think of some specific ways in which the Old Testament Scriptures will be useful to us in the New Earth, when there is no longer any sin?

It will reveal aspects of God's infinite character, and probably infinitely (and forever) so. And for that reason, it will be a crucial and indispensable constant reference for reading and discussion.

90. **Question for you:** Do you think God requires you to remember the things you asked Him for long ago in order for Him to continue working out their fulfillment? In other words, are there some prayers you made long ago that God is still answering even though you have forgotten that you ever asked Him for those petitions?

No (to the first question). Yes (to the second question).

91. **Question for you:** This octet is, in part, a response to the previous octet. How is the enduring applicability of the Laws of YHWH an encouraging answer to the severe agony expressed in the previous octet (vv. 81-88)?

God's omniscient faithfulness is an encouragement in my trials because I know that even if I can't see a satisfactory resolution to my afflictions, God can and does.

92. **Question for you:** Do you think God is interested in our obedience to His Law from a sense of duty? Or is He only interested when we obey from a sense of delight in His Law?

I think only when our obedience is an expression of our <u>trust</u> in Him and His goodness.

93. **Question for you:** If the Laws of YHWH are forever applicable and important, then what is the meaning of Colossians 2:14 when it says, God "cancelled the written code, with its regulations, that was against us and that stood opposed to us; he took it away, nailing it to the cross"?

The written code (given through Moses) is no longer used to measure our righteousness (if we are in Christ), but it is still a true statement of the character of God.

94. **Question for you:** If Jesus "sought out" the Precepts of YHWH, then does that searching imply that there were things to understand about YHWH's Precepts that Jesus did not yet understand?

Yes.

95. **Question for you:** Can you list some of the ways in which Jesus has freed you from the <u>effects</u> of sin and evil? *NOTE: In your answer, it would be helpful to list things other than your behaviors (other than your actions and activities).*

1. *Reduction of hopelessness in my life*
2. *Less fear*
3. *Less guilt*

96. **Questions for you:**

When your life begins to fall apart and you desperately need something steady and stable to hold onto, do you ever consider that you might find that needed stability in the Commands of God? What would that look like for you?

Yes. Hold on to obedience to the commands of God and avoid catastrophe.

Often we think of the Commands of God as being the Ten Commandments, but there are many other Commands of God in Scripture. For example, can you list the Commands of God that appear in the first chapter of the Book of Genesis? (We count at least 22 specific "spoken by God" Commands.)

- *Let there be light.*
- *Let the seas teem with creatures.*
- *Let the sky be filled with birds.*
- *Let them bring forth according to their kind.*
- *Etc.*

97. **Question for you:** Do you find it surprising that the reason Jesus constantly meditates on the Law of YHWH is because He is in love?

A new thought, but not surprising.

98. **Question for you:** Have you ever considered that an effective way to become more successful in life is to learn and apply more of the Commands of God?

I heard a Jewish taxi driver in NYC say this to me one time. (That was about 50 years ago.)

99. **Question for you:** Do you trust more in the Statutes and Testimonies of God than you do in your own experiences? How would Jesus answer this question?

It is a mixed bag for me, but Jesus has answered "always yes" to this question.

100. **Question for you:** What would a college curriculum look like that was focused exclusively on discovering the insights buried in Scripture and then teaching how to apply those in all the different challenges of everyday life?

It would look like what the Church and church ought to be.

101. **Question for you:** How does John 8:28 confirm the above statement?

Jesus didn't need (even refused) to learn anything other than what YHWH instructed Him to know and say.

102. **Question for you:** In light of the roles outlined above, how is it that The Father would call The Son His (The Father's) God (as He does in Hebrews 1:8)?

Extreme love. What we love most is our God.

103. **Question for you:** Do the Ten Commandments seem like a love letter to you?

It's getting to be more so all the time.

104. **Question for you:** Is it possible to find true and useful understanding from any source that does not align with the word of God? What aligns with the word of God better than Scripture?

Jesus aligns perfectly with the Precepts of YHWH. "No" to the first question, and "nothing" to the second one.

105. **Question for you:** When you find yourself thinking (and feeling) that you are more righteous when you are obedient to the word of God, do you realize that faulty thinking is a natural error that comes from your fallen nature? Have you noticed that when you are walking by the Spirit (your new nature) that you are not inclined to think (or feel) such things?

Yes. Yes.

106. **Question for you:** When Christians think they achieve greater righteousness through their obedience to the Laws of God, what does that imply about their opinion of the sufficiency of what was provided to them by Christ?

That it was not complete and therefore not sufficient.

107. **Question for you:** What causes you to mourn?

I wrote all about it in the commentary to v. 107.

108. **Question for you:** Do you understand that when you obey the Laws of God, your obedience is a gift from God to you, and it is **NOT** a gift from you to God?

Absolutely!

109. **Question for you:** How do you think it felt for Jesus to have His life constantly being put at risk? (Note: This is not a rhetorical question.)

Some thrilling. Some mourning.

110. **Question for you:** In the above paragraph, what is the reason given for why we would want to "consistently walk in accordance to the Precepts of YHWH"?

Because we are already completely justified.

111. **Question for you:** Is it possible to love God and not love His Laws?

Not for long.

112. **Question for you:** Is it possible that, even in heaven, Jesus is engaged in a never ending process of continually increasing His experiential intimacy with His Father?

From our non-infinite perspective: probably.

113. **Question for you:** I, and every other person who is in Christ, is a double-minded person—at least in this life. But Jesus does not hate me; in fact, it is quite the opposite. How do you explain the fact that Jesus hates double-mindedness, but He loves me (and you)?

He hates how it robs us of an abundant life.

114. **Question for you:** Why and how does the word of God stop the world's most powerful people "dead in their tracks"?

It exposes the weakness of their argument and publicly embarrasses them such that they dare not continue their attack. In essence, their attack ends up with the realization that they have laid a snare for themselves, and if they continue, they will fall into their own trap.

115. **Question for you:** Have you ever noticed that when wicked people implement solutions that align with the Commands of God, that it works out well for them? And when Christians implement solutions that do not align with the Commands of God, that those solutions do not work in the long run?

Yes. It is still puzzling, though. How can a solution be implemented so that it aligns with the Commands of God without God being part of the implementation? Is this an aspect of His common grace?

116. **Question for you:** The point in Jesus' life when He was most publicly humiliated and shamed was when He was stripped naked, beaten, and crucified in the company of known criminals. Why then do we now publicly and proudly display crosses as adorning jewelry?

This was His greatest hour. It was our highest example of love and nobility. It was God at His most majestic. So, we acknowledge this testimony with our adorning jewelry.

117. **Question for you:** Have you come to the point, yet, where you realize that your faith is not effective because of how hard you believe, but it is effective because of how powerful and faithful God is to do what He has promised?

I think, mostly, yes.

118. **Question for you:** Have you ever gotten something you really wanted and worked hard for, only to have it end up not being very satisfying in the end? Is that because it was not aligned with the Statutes of God?

Yes. Yes.

119. **Question for you:** Have you ever viewed the Statutes of God as predictors of success?

No, but it is a good thought!

120. **Question for you:** Does it frighten you to think about doing something in your life that does not align with the Laws of God as they are written in Scripture?

It does, and more so all the time.

121. **Question for you:** What does it mean to be arrogant?

It means to think you have a better way than that which is prescribed by God in His word/Word.

122. **Question for you:** Do you see that if you believe that "doing your best to do good will be acceptable to God," then you are one of the arrogant; you are delusional; and you justly deserve the coming wrath of God—unless you change your thinking about how you become acceptable to God (because it is certainly not by doing your best to do good)?

Yes to all of this.

123. &

124. **Question for you:** How would your life be different if you began to refuse to solve life's puzzles as best you could, but instead, continually relied only on God's provisions as the Holy Spirit reveals them to you when you read His word?

For one thing, I would have to spend a lot more time in the word and in prayer seeking God's direction for all the details of my life.

125. **Question for you:** Does it seem to you that experientially knowing the Testimonies and Statutes of God is a good way to get to experientially know God Himself?

   Yes. Is this the primary way we are to fulfill John 17:3?

126. **Question for you:** What action was Jesus' requesting of His Father as the appropriate immediate response to YHWH's Law being broken?

   To fully equip the Christ and divinely provide for His efficacious repudiation of Satan's proposition by demonstrating the reasonableness of the incarnate Son of Man living according to the word of YHWH.

127. **Question for you:** What else did Jesus say about this—what do the next two verses say that follow Matthew 5:17?

   We who are in Christ should make it a priority to teach the Commands of YHWH to others.

128. **Question for you:** If John 17:3 means that the only thing that really matters is getting to experientially know God and Jesus Christ whom He has sent, then why would you even want to ever consider anything apart from the Precepts of God?

   This stance seems to require extensive (and non-natural) insight into the word of God. For example, it requires one to (eventually) discover all of mathematics (see Gödel's incompleteness theorem for the magnitude of this effort), all of Physics, and all of true science as corollaries of the Law of God as revealed in the Scriptures. It would require a complete commitment to the first several verses of the Book of Proverbs. It would require the proper understanding and digesting of all of the New Testament as rules by which one is to live life wisely in Christ. It would require ... (So, these are some of the things I suspect I will be doing in the New Earth.)

129. **Question for you:** If you are in Christ, does that have any implication on the importance of the things you focus your attention on? (See Romans 6 for more discussion on this

thought.)

The things we pay attention to are the things the children of God, indwelt with the Holy Spirit, have deemed worthy of the attention of Jesus Christ.

130. **Question for you:** Is it possible to be wise apart from the spoken word of YHWH as it is written in the Scriptures and unfolded to us by the Holy Spirit?

No. Wisdom is living the will of God according to the mind of Christ. This requires God's active participation and provision.

131. **Question for you:** Some people think that "walking in the Spirit" is the same thing as, or at least is indistinguishable from, having a strong **affinity** for the Testimonies of YHWH as recorded in Scripture. What do you think about this?

Yes, but they need to be understood and apprehended in the fuller context of the Person of Jesus Christ. We who are indwelt by the Holy Spirit have a strong affinity for Christ as He is revealed to us in the Scriptures, which is, in part, in complete alignment with the Law of God.

132. **Question for you:** Have you ever considered it an act of divine mercy when God allows you to read His word?

Yes! Isn't it gloriously marvelous that God would share His thoughts and provision to us through His written word?

133. **Question for you:** Do you yet realize that "doing your best to do good" is the height of rebellion against God? How does "doing your best to do good" fit into Genesis 3:1-7?

Yes. "Doing my best to do good" is the arrogant rejection of the truth that "only my Father in heaven is good."

134. **Question for you:** Have you ever felt oppressed? Have you ever thought that this could be caused by being functionally disconnected from the word of God?

Yes. I'm working on it.

135. **Question for you:** Do you want more light in your life? According to this verse, where do you go to get it?

Yes. I get more light from God as He reveals Himself in His Statutes.

136. **Question for you:** Do you ever feel like keeping the Law of God is a burden? If so, according to the above commentary, what two things are you failing to accept that causes you to feel that burden?

Yes.
1. *Jesus is the Law Keeper and He has kept the Law for us. So, I am not condemned by God when I fail to keep it properly.*
2. *The Law is good and is the merciful goodness of God revealed to me in practical ways.*

137. **Question for you:** When you think about the Laws of God as contained in the Bible, have you ever wanted to celebrate and bust out in grateful praise to God for giving us something that is always right and true and good?

For me, this is a new perspective on the Law of God. Before this, I never thought of them as an anchor for sanity in an insane world.

138. **Question for you:** Are you getting the picture that Jesus really, really, REALLY loves the Commandments of YHWH?

Yes! And He is leading me to really, really, REALLY love the Commandments of YHWH!

139. **Question for you:** Do you mourn when you see those you care about ignoring the counsel of Scripture?

Yes. It gives me a sense of hopelessness for them and their condition. They may be saved, but they relegate themselves to a life of vain searchings and misery, when what Jesus wants to give them through His word is an abundant life full of joy, peace and the blessings of the Lord.

140. **Question for you:** Do you think you will ever get to the point where the possession you most treasure on earth (in this life) is the word of God?

I sure hope so! Please, Lord Jesus, let it be so!

141. **Question for you:** Does God withhold any good thing from you? How much good does He provide for you through His Precepts? How many of those good provisions has Jesus already earned for you?

No, God does not withhold any good thing from me. He provides an unimaginable amount of good to me through His Precepts. Jesus has earned it ALL for me (and my brothers and sisters).

142. **Question for you:** Do you take solace in knowing that the Laws of YHWH are unmovable, unflexing eternal statements of absolute truth?

Yes. Jesus is my rock; and the word of YHWH is my rock. For me, Jesus is the Word of YHWH (John 1).

143. **Question for you:** What is the best way for you to respond to the fact that Jesus found great hope and delight in the Commands of YHWH?

I need to follow my Lord and ask God to lead me to find great hope and delight in His Commands. May it be so, Father, as the Lord Jesus Christ has provided by His finished work!

144. **Question for you:** If living by the Statutes and Testimonies of YHWH do not make us better Christians, and since they also do not gain us greater favor or approval in God's sight, then why should we embrace them?

   Because Jesus loved them and embraced them, and I want to love and embrace the things that Jesus loved and embraced!

145. **Question for you:** Do you ever try to obey the Commands of God in your own strength? Is that relying on God to provide your righteousness?

   Yes (in answer to the first question). No (in answer to the second question).

146. **Question for you:** Did Jesus completely fulfill all the requirements for you to now be seen as perfectly right in God's sight? Is there anything left for you to fulfill?

   Yes (in answer to the first question). No (in answer to the second question).

147. **Question for you:** Do you ever find yourself fervently crying out to God even though you already know He is going to provide what you ask? Why do you do that? Why did Jesus do that?

   Yes, more and more often, the older I get. I do that because the saliency of my need continues to increase. I think maybe Jesus did that for the same reason.

148. **Question for you:** What are some things/activities in your life that function according to an established frequency (or cycle time)?

   Eating, breathing, heart beating, sleeping, prayer time while reading Scripture, personal hygiene, ...

149. **Question for you:** Do you ever get delivered from trouble apart from God doing it as prescribed in His word?

   Probably not.

150.
and

151. **Question for you:** Would you rather have the friendship of God, or the friendship of some other person? (This is not asking which you should prefer; it is asking which you actually do prefer.)

I would rather have the friendship of God!

152. **Question for you:** What is it about having Jesus be your best friend that makes that be an undesirable proposition for you?

Constant conviction—but even that is becoming a desirable state for me. Holy Spirit, I thank you that you are constantly and faithfully doing corrective surgery on my soul.

153. **Question for you:** Jesus said, "Blessed are those who mourn, for they shall be comforted." If you were to ask Jesus how He received His suffering, affliction, and mourning, do you think He would say, "I'm glad for it all because then I get to experience the deliverance and comfort of YHWH"?

Yes, I think that is exactly what He would say.

154. **Question for you:** In the original Hebrew, Jesus often refers to the word of YHWH as the "spoken word" of YHWH. What percent of the time would you guess that "spoken word" came to Jesus in the form of the written word in the Old Testament Scriptures?

Not 100%, because God spoke at Jesus' baptism; but I think it was probably a very high percentage of the time that Jesus received the "spoken word" of God from the Scriptures.

155. **Question for you:** If someone gave you a lifetime membership in a very exclusive club in which the members were provided (free) all sorts of exciting wholesome activities and delicious healthy foods, would you use that membership often? Do you see that Jesus has purchased for you that sort of membership in the club of those who are allowed to live according to the Laws of YHWH without fear of any type of condemnation or personal criticism?

Yes, thank you, Lord Jesus, for giving me an eternal irrevocable membership in God's club of provisions.

156. **Question for you:** Do you see the judgments of God as tender mercies? Did Jesus see them that way? (See the Hebrew Literal for v. 156.)

Yes, the judgments of God are all tender mercies. Yes.

157. **Question for you:** Where do you get your righteousness from? <u>All</u> of it?

I get my righteousness only from the finished work of Christ.

158. **Question for you:** What do you conclude when Scripture tells us one thing and modern science (or even our own observations) tell us the exact opposite? Which source do you trust to have the correct answer?

I need to trust God's word more than I trust my own (or others') observations and experiences.

159. **Question for you:** Do you understand that in order for the Statutes of YHWH to be efficacious, they require the continual personal intervention of YHWH?

Yes, and <u>PRAISE GOD</u> that they do, because interacting with God and His sent Son is the only thing that has any value.

160. **Question for you:** Is the Law of God your friend?

The Law of God is my friend!

161. **Question for you:** If you are in Christ, do you recognize that God has written His Laws on your heart, and when you are walking by the Spirit, that affinity emerges?

Yes.

162. **Question for you:** What do you value more than deepening your relationship with God? (You can tell by whatever gives you greater delight than deepening your relationship with God.)

I don't like to think about this question. I don't like searching for, or admitting, its answers.

163. **Question for you:** What in your life is not aligned with the word and will of God? (You can tell by what you are willing to lie about, or at least prefer to remain hidden.)

Ouch!

164. **Question for you:** Does this suggest anything to you?

I have tried to pray an octet every four hours. I don't seem to be able to keep it up for very long.

165. **Question for you:** Do you want more peace in your life? How did Jesus get peace in His life? (See v.165)

Yes, I want more peace in my life. Jesus got peace by relying on YHWH to lead Him through life according to His Laws and Precepts.

166. **Question for you:** Have you ever before realized that acting in opposition to the Statutes of YHWH is psychotic? That it is a form of insanity?

No. No, but I can now see how it is insane.

167. **Question for you:** Did you realize that getting your soul's needs met by things in this world is a characteristic of your fallen nature; versus getting your soul's needs met by the very Person of God is characteristic of your new nature in Christ?

Yes.

Also, have you realized that when you are getting your soul's needs met by seeking the face of God that you are walking by the Spirit; versus when you are getting your soul's needs met by things in this physical world that you are walking by the flesh?

I do now.

168. **Question for you:** According to this Psalm 119, what could you do to take greater advantage of the provisions and benefits God has for you? (Hint: It does not involve trying harder to do anything.)

Rely more on the roadmap laid out in the Precepts and Testimonies of God's word.

169. **Question for you:** Is it possible for a person to get true understanding of the word of God without having God reveal its truth to them?

No, that is not possible.

170. **Question for you:** What is the ultimate outcome when you are apparently delivered from trouble, but it is not in accordance with the word of God?

Train wreck! Futility. Illusion. Delusion.

171. **Question for you:** In your own words, what is the "dual-role dynamic" described in the above paragraph?

The Father's role is to show His will through His word and to lead us through the implementation of that in our lives. It is our role to accept no other solution.

172. **Question for you:** Without using the words "righteousness" or "right," in your own words describe what it means when this verse (v. 172) says, "all your commands are righteous."

All of God's Commands prescribe exactly what we need in order to have the perfect solution for every situation we will face in life.

173. **Question for you:** If you decide to follow the Precepts of God in some given situation, according to this verse, what else do you have to do to experience a successful outcome?

God has to lead us through the proper application of that/those Precept(s) for that particular situation.

174. **Question for you:** Whose salvation was a stake in this verse?

Mine and my brothers' and sisters'.

175. **Question for you:** Have you yet come to view the judgments of God as your faithful helpers?

Merciful, all-knowing, pure, right, faithful helpers—yes.

176. **Question for you:** How would you explain to a non-Christian what it means to "accept the offer," in words they would understand? This often means you cannot use "religious" words (such as "saved," "faith," "sin," etc.), because other people will not understand or define these words as you do.

Because we have rebelled against God and His will for our lives, we have lost the approval of God. Instead of approval from God, our rebellion has earned His wrath and judgment—whether we like it or not. (continued on next page)

Jesus, by always desiring to be in complete alignment with God's stated will, has earned God's complete approval as well as all the blessings that come with that complete approval.

After earning that approval and those blessings, Jesus loved us so much that He volunteered to exchange, with us, that approval and those blessings in exchange for the wrath and judgment we had earned. So, the wrath and judgment we deserved was poured out from God onto Jesus when He was crucified on the cross, so we might have in exchange the approval and blessings that Jesus had earned. But to have these, we must acknowledge the exchange and accept it.

Made in the USA
Monee, IL
27 November 2021

83198340R00109